SONGS THAT TEACH

Beth Black
Susan H. Kenney
Patricia Haglund Nielsen
Rosalie R. Pratt

EDEN HILL

Contents

Preface

This collection contains a variety of folk songs, including many well-known American and foreign favorites. They are of particular value not only for the enjoyment they create, but also for the musical concepts and skills that classroom teachers and children can explore through them. They are versatile songs that can be accompanied, harmonized, danced and analyzed, and are considered an important part of our musical heritage. We invite you to explore the world of joy found in this collection.

Appreciation is expressed to *Richards Institute of Music Education and Research* for permission to reprint "Circle Left," "Ginger Snap," "Bodling," "Kitty Kitty Casket," "Maple Swamp," "Penny Song," "Rain Rain," "Sally Go Round the Sun," "Going Down the Railroad," and "You Turn . . . I Turn" from *Aesthetic Foundations for Thinking: Part III*, by Mary Helen Richards, ©1980; "Clickety Clack," "Come and Follow Me," "Hickety, Tickety Bumblebee," "High Stepping Horses," and "Johnny Hold Your Hand Up" from *Experience Games Through Music*, by Fleurette Sweeney and Margaret Wharram, ©1973; "Frog's In the Meadow," "Windy Weather," and "Yonder She Comes" from *Music Language 1*, by Mary Helen Richards, ©1973; and "Ground Hog" from *Music Language 2*, by Mary Helen Richards, ©1974.

Other copyright information is given below each song where applicable.

Reference to *The Heritage Songster* by Leon and Lynn Dallin (Wm. C. Brown Company Publishers) is abbreviated H.S. throughout.

A Ram Sam Sam

A ram sam sam, A ram sam sam, Gu-li gu-li gu-li gu-li gu-li ram sam sam.

A ra fi, A ra fi, Gu-li gu-li gu-li gu-li gu-li ram sam sam.

Encourage the children to use hand signs or to play on resonator bells the following patterns as they occur in the song.

Ask the children to sing the above patterns in their heads as they hand sign.

After School

When school is out we go home and then Les - sons we've learned we'll

stu - dy a - gain. "Good - bye" to teach - ers and friends we say.

we'll see each oth - er on a bright new day.

This song is based on the pentatonic scale — G A B D E. Any of these tones may be combined into a simple 2, 3, or 4 note ostinato to sing or play as an accompaniment. For example:

School is out ___ School is out ___

Because this song is pentatonic, it may be played on the black keys of the piano beginning on B flat.

Aiken Drum

1. There was a man lived in the moon, lived in the moon, lived in the moon
2. And the played u-pon a la - dle, a la - dle, a la - dle

There was a man lived in the moon and his name was Ai - ken Drum.
And he played u - pon a la - dle, and his name was Ai - ken Drum.

Invite some children to sing and hand sign these ostinati or play them on resonator bells to accompany the song.

mi fa mi re mi fa mi re do

do la sol sol do la sol sol do

Feel the beat, the rhythmic pattern, and the accent with different body movements.

Work in partners. One person keeps beat by himself while his partner keeps song pattern on person's back. Trade.

Ain't That a Rockin' All Night

Traditional South Carolina

REFRAIN

Now ain't that a rock - in' all night____

Now ain't that a rock - in' all night

Now ain't that a rock - in' all night____ All night long.

-2-

1. Mar - y   and___ the lit - tle Ba - by,   Born in Beth - le - hem,
2. Mar - y   called___ the Ba - by Je - sus,   He was the Son of God,

D.C. al Fine

Ev - 'ry time___ the   Ba - by cry,___ She   rock - in' the wear - y Lamb.
Just like any___ other Ba - by child,_ She   sing Him a rock - in' song.

The refrain of this song is harmonized in parallel sixths below the melody. Let children discover two places where the harmony is a fifth below rather than a sixth.

The Allee-Allee O

Traditional

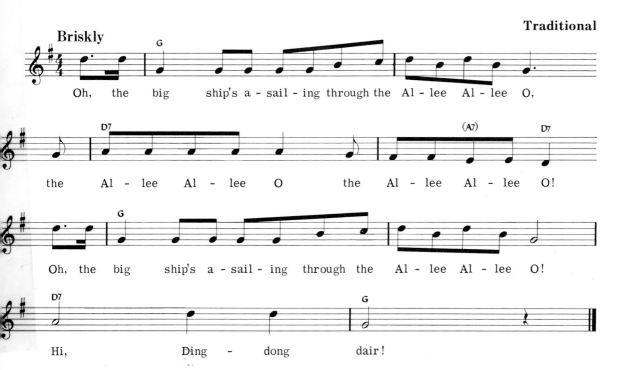

Briskly

Oh, the big   ship's a - sail - ing through the Al - lee Al - lee O,

the   Al - lee Al - lee O   the Al - lee Al - lee O!

Oh, the big   ship's a - sail - ing through the Al - lee Al - lee O!

Hi,   Ding - dong   dair!

The Allee is a channel between large rocks off the coast of Maine.

Help the children make up additional verses to this song: "Oh the sailboat is sailing down the Allee-Allee O," etc.

Make charts of the melodic patterns of the words "Allee-Allee O." Help the children discover which pattern is sung first, second, and last.

Amen

Afro-American Canon

A - - - men, a - - - men,

a - - - - men, a - men, a - men.

The Angel Band

Folk Song from South Carolina

VERSE

There was one there were two, there were three lit - tle an - gels,

There were four, there were five, there were six lit - tle an - gels,

There were seven, there were eight, there were nine lit - tle an - gels,

Ten lit tle___ an - gels in the band._____

REFRAIN

Oh, was - n't that a band, Sun - day morn - ing,

Sun - day morn - ing, Sun - day morn - ing?

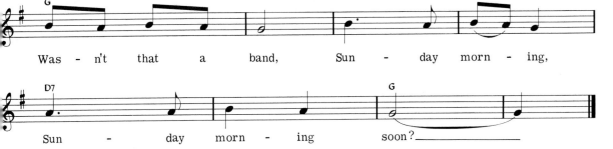

Was - n't that a band, Sun - day morn - ing,

Sun - day morn - ing soon?

This song is based on the pentatonic scale G A B D E. Any of these tones may be combined into a simple 2, 3, or 4 note ostinato to sing or play as an accompaniment. For example:

Lit - tle an - gels— Lit - tle an - gels—

OR

lay the ti ti ta rhythm pattern each time it occurs in the verse of the song.

The Animal Fair

With humor   **Traditional**

I went to the an - i - mal fair,___ The birds and the beasts were there.___

The old rac-coon by the light of the moon Was comb-ing her au - burn hair.___

The fun - ni-est was the monk,___ He climbed up the el - e-phant's trunk,___

The el - e - phant sneezed and fell on his knees, And what be-came of the monk?___

Try playing the following ostinato on resonator bells, or invite part of the class to sing it to accompany the song.

The monk, the monk, the monk the monk,

Help the children find the following tonal pattern in the song, and invite the class to hand sign that pattern or play it on resonator bells each time it is sung.

La La

Sol Sol Sol   Sol

Mi   Mi

- 5 -

As I Roved Out

Newfoundland Folk Song

Briskly

1. As	I roved out one fine sum-mer's eve - nin',	
2. Saying: "Daugh - ter, oh daugh - ter, I'll have you to mar - ry,	
3. "A sail - or boy thinks all for to wan - der;	
4. "Oh, moth - er, I cannot wed with a farm - er,	

To view the flow'rs and to take the air,
No long - er to lead a sweet sin - gle life."
And he will prove your o - ver - throw.
Al - though he deck me with di - a - monds bright,

'Twas there I spied a ten - der moth - er
"Oh moth - er, oh moth - er, I'd ra - ther to tar - ry To
Oh daugh - ter, you're bet - ter to wed with a farm - er,
I'll wait for my love with the tar - ry striped trou - sers, For

Talk - in' to her daugh - ter dear.
be some brave young sail - or's wife."
For to the seas he ne'er do go."
he's my joy and my heart's de - light."

Although this song is chorded in D minor, it is sung in the Dorian Mode because there is no B flat.

Banua

This is a chant from Johannesburg, South Africa. There is a large stadium there which holds about fifty thousand people. Often they will begin singing this chant in the stadium as loudly as they possibly can. Then with each repetition they will sing softer and softer until they are barely humming.

Behold That Star

Spiritual

Moderate speed

Be - hold that star,___ Be - hold that star up yon - der,

Be - hold that star,___ It is the star of Beth - le - hem,___ *Fine*

1. There was no room found in the inn,___
2. The wise men tra - velled from the East,___ It is the star of Beth - le - hem,___
3. A song broke forth up - on the night,___

For Him who was born___ free from sin.___
To wor - ship___ Him, the Prince of Peace.___ It is the star of Beth - le - hem___ O
From an - gel___ hosts all robed in white.___

Consider dramatizing this song as a short Christmas play.

The Bells in the Steeple

Carl Orff

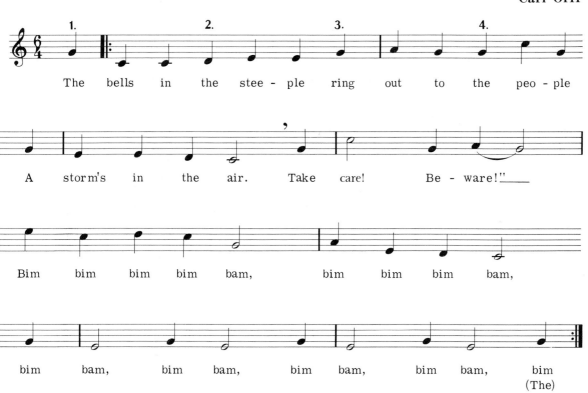

The bells in the stee - ple ring out to the peo - ple
A storm's in the air. Take care! Be - ware!"___
Bim bim bim bim bam, bim bim bim bam,
bim bam, bim bam, bim bam, bim bam, bim
(The)

...ing in canon. Accompany the singing by playing the following ostinati on Orff instruments or resonator bells:

Soprano-Xylophone

Alto-Xylophone

Gamba

Timpani

Bluebird, Bluebird

Texas Folk Song

Blue - bird, blue - bird, go through my win - dow,

Blue - bird, blue - bird, go through my win - dow,

Blue - bird, blue - bird, go through my win - dow,

and buy mo - lass - es can - dy.

Take a lit - tle (girl/boy) and tap (her/him) on the shoul - der,

Take a lit - tle (girl/boy) and tap (her/him) on the shoul - der,

Take a lit - tle (girl/boy) and tap (her/him) on the shoul - der,

and buy mo - lass - es can - dy.

Encourage the children to use hand signs or to play on resonator bells or piano the following patterns as they occur in the song.

OR

Sol Mi Sol Mi Sol La Sol Mi   Sol Fa Mi Re Do Do

This song may be sung as a partner song with "He's Got the Whole World in His Hands" (H.S., p. 206), "Polly Put the Kettle On," "Rocka My Soul," "Sandy Land" (H.S., p. 107), "Skip to My Lou" (H.S., p. 232), "Ten Little Indians" (H.S., p. 163), and "Where Oh Where Is Pretty Little Susie?"

Bodling

1. Bodl-ing, Bodl-ing, Bodl-ing, Bodl-ing, Bodl-ing, Bodl-ing, Link-a - do.
2. Bodl-ing, Bodl-ing, Bodl-ing, Bodl-ing, Bodl-ing, Bodl-ing, Link-a - dive.
3. Bodl-ing, Bodl-ing, Bodl-ing, Bodl-ing, Bodl-ing, Bodl-ing, Link-a - doad.

Bodl-ing, Bodl-ing, Bodl-ing, Bodl-ing, Bodl-ing, Bodl-ing, Link - a - do.
Bodl-ing, Bodl-ing, Bodl-ing, Bodl-ing, Bodl-ing, Bodl-ing, Link - a - dive.
Bodl-ing, Bodl-ing, Bodl-ing, Bodl-ing, Bodl-ing, Bodl-ing, Link - a - doad.

Link - a - do and a mer-ry go too, Link -a - do and a mer-ry go too.
Link - a - dive and a sakes alive, Link -a - dive and a sakes a - live.
Link - a - doad and a tum-bl - ing toad, Link -a - doad and a tum - bl - ing toad.

I'll bet a man a brand new shoe that there are on-ly thirty-two.
I'll bet a boy a big bee-hive that there are real-ly only five.
I'll give a girl a ring of gold to sing the mix-o-ly-di-an mode.

This song is sung in the mixolydian mode. Its tonal center is G, but there is no F sharp.

Chatter with the Angels

Chat-ter with the an-gels soon in the morn-ing; Chat-ter with the an-gels in that land.

Chat-ter with the an - gels soon in the morn-ing; Chat-ter with the an-gels; Join that band.

I want to join that band and chat-ter with the an - gels all day long.

I want to join that band and chat-ter with the an - gels all day long.

Invite children to use hand signs or to play on resonator bells the *Mi Re Do* pattern each time it occurs in the song.

Mi Re Do

Create different body movements for each phrase.

Chester

Majestically
William Billings

1. Let ty - rants shake their i - - ron rod
2. What grate - ful off - 'ring shall___ we bring,

And slav - 'ry clank___ her gall - - ing chains;
What shall we ren - - der to___ the Lord?

We fear them not, We___ trust___ in God;
Loud Hal - le - lu - jahs___ let___ us sing,

New___ Eng - land's God___ for - ev - - er reigns.
And___ praise His name___ on ev - - 'ry chord.

William Billings is an Early American composer of the Revolutionary Era.

William Schumann has used the song "Chester" in an orchestral theme and variations in one movement of his *New England Triptych*. Let the children discover how Mr. Schumann has changed the song in his composition.

Children, Go Where I Send You

Traditional

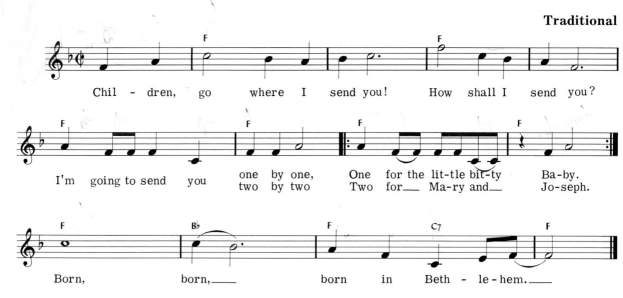

Chil - dren, go where I send you! How shall I send you?

I'm going to send you one by one, One for the lit-tle bit-ty Ba-by.
two by two Two for__ Ma-ry and__ Jo-seph.

Born, born,__ born in Beth - le - hem.__

Three for the wise men riding

Four for the gospel makers

Five for the friendly beasts watching

Six for the shepherds who were kneeling

Seven for the seven mighty angels

Circle Left

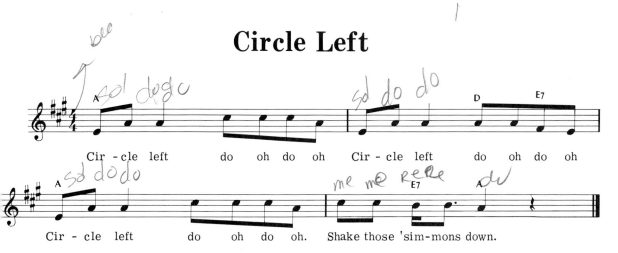

Cir - cle left   do   oh   do   oh   Cir - cle left   do   oh   do   oh

Cir - cle left   do   oh   do   oh.   Shake those 'sim-mons down.

Transpose to the key of C (begin on G) and sing as a partner song with "Penny Song."

Help the children discover the *Sol₁ Do Do* pattern in this song. Invite them to sing and hand sign the pattern or play on resonator bells each time it occurs in the song.

Sol₁   Do   Do

Play on rhythm instruments and sing the rhythm pattern ti   ti   ta each time it occurs.

Make a chart of the ti dem rhythm pattern. Help children discover on which word it occurs. Ask children to sing the word in their heads while they clap or play that rhythm on an instrument. Find the same rhythm pattern in "Maple Swamp," "Penny Song," "Rain, Rain," and "Happy Is the Miller."

This pentatonic song may be played on the black notes of the piano beginning on C sharp.

Circle Round the Zero

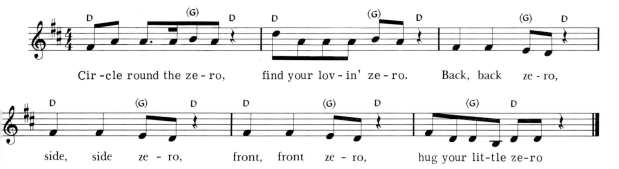

Cir -cle round the ze - ro,   find your lov - in' ze - ro.   Back, back   ze - ro,

side,   side   ze - ro,   front, front   ze - ro,   hug your lit - tle ze - ro

Partner game: Partners face each other. Each partner circles clockwise and halfway until both are back to back. Touch shoulders on "back, back." Continue another quarter circle and touch left arms on "side, side." Complete circle and slap partner's palms for "front, front."

Repeat game and vary by singing parts of song (e.g. "back back zero") in your head.

This song could be played as a one-chord song.

Clickety Clack

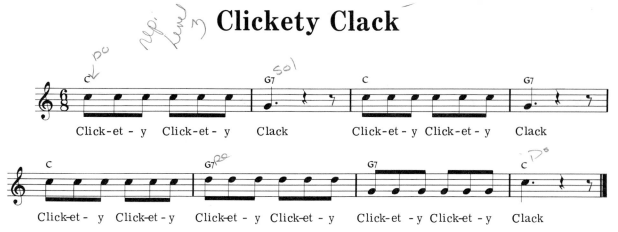

Click-et - y Click-et - y Clack   Click-et - y Click-et - y Clack

Click-et - y Click-et - y   Click-et - y Click-et - y   Click-et - y Click-et - y Clack

This song uses only 3 tones: C, D, and G (*Do Re* and *Sol*₁). Sing with hand signs. Play the resonator bells at the beginning of each measure to outline melody while singing:

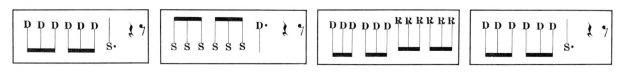

Sing as a canon.

Write the rhythm and tone syllables of each measure on charts, then mix them up and invite children to correct the measure order or change the song by singing it in mixed order.

Come and Follow Me

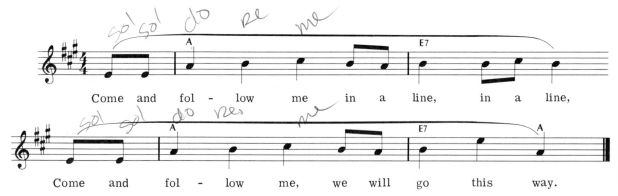

Come   and   fol - low   me   in   a   line,   in   a   line,

Come   and   fol - low   me,   we   will   go   this   way.

After playing the game invite children to find the following pattern in the song. Hand sign or play the pattern on resonator bells each time it occurs.

Sol₁   Sol₁   Do   Re   Mi

Play on instruments and sing the rhythm pattern ti ti   ta each time it occurs.

Make up other verses to this tune. "Come and clap with me" etc. "Come and jump with me" etc.

Come, Follow, Follow

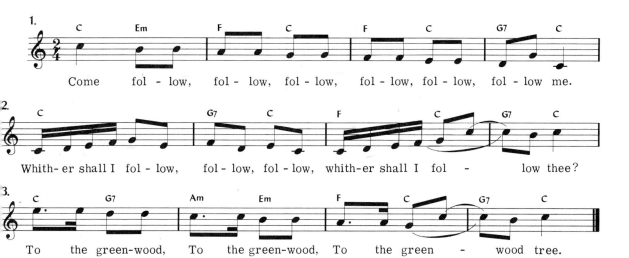

1. Come fol - low, fol - low, fol - low, fol - low, fol - low, fol - low me.

2. Whith- er shall I fol - low, fol - low, fol - low, whith-er shall I fol - low thee?

3. To the green-wood, To the green-wood, To the green - wood tree.

If you sing this song as a round, repeat the chords of the **first phrase** for each line.

Da Pacem Domine

PART 1

Reverently

By Melchior Franck

Da pa-cem Do - mi-ne, da pa-cem Do - mi-ne in di - e-bus nos - tris.

Part 2 begins 2 beats later and a fourth lower than part 1.

PART 2

Da pa-cem Do - mi - ne, Da pa-cem Do - mi - ne in di-e-bus nos - tris.

This Latin canon dates from 1600. The words mean "give us peace oh Lord."

In some old canons, the rhythm of the second part is altered to catch up with the first part. Such is the case in this canon.

Daddy Shot a Bear

Alabama

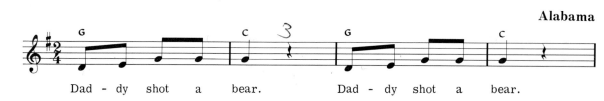

Dad - dy shot a bear.   Dad - dy shot a bear.

Shot him through a key - hole and nev - er touched a hair!   hair!

This little song has only three tones: D, E, and G (*Sol, La,* and *Do*). Encourage children to hand sign as they sing and to play the song on resonator bells or piano.

This song may be accompanied with only the G chord.

Make up other verses: "Daddy feeds the bear,
Daddy feeds the bear
Daddy feeds the bear because he loves him so."

The Day is Now Over

Carl Orff

The day is now o - ver the moon shines so bright,

lit - tle chil - dren are pray - ing for care through the night.

Then our heav - en - ly Fa - ther throws o - pen the gate

and sends down His an - gels to watch o'er their fate.

Sing in canon. Accompany the singing by playing the following ostinati on Orff instruments or resonator bells:

Do, Lord

Down Came a Lady

Virginia Folk Song

Down came a la - dy, down came two,

Down came Sa - ra Ann and she was dressed in blue.

Make up other verses.

Let children play this song on bells, water glasses, or pop bottles. You will need only three bells: F, G, and A.

Draw a Bucket of Water

Georgia

Draw a buck - et of wa - ter for my neigh - bor's daugh - ter.

One in a rush two in a rush first old [man lady] pops un - der.

The game is played in groups of four children, two holding hands outstretched, while the other couple joins hands across the first couple's. The couples stand in place, pumping their joined hands up and down in time to the music. At the end of the stanza, a boy or girl "pops under" the joined hands crossed in front, without letting go, so that there is first one child enclosed in the center, then two, then three, then four. Finally, with the last child, a basket has been formed by the interlocking arms behind the waists of all the children.

The Drunken Sailor

VERSE

1. What shall we do with the drunk - en sail - or,
2. Put him in the long - boat till he's so - ber,

What shall we do with the drunk - en sail - or,
Put him in the long - boat till he's so - ber,

What shall we do with the drunk - en sail - or,
Put him in the long - boat till he's so - ber, Ear - lye in the morn - ing.

REFRAIN

Way hey and up she ri - ses, Way hey and up she ri - ses,

Way hey and up she ri - ses, Ear - lye in the morn - ing.

Although this song is chorded in D minor, it is sung in the Dorian Mode because there is no B flat.

3. Pull out the plug and wet him all over,
   Pull out the plug and wet him all over,
   Pull out the plug and wet him all over,
   Earlye in the morning.

4. Put him in the scuppers with a hose-pipe on him,
   Put him in the scuppers with a hose-pipe on him,
   Put him in the scuppers with a hose-pipe on him,
   Earlye in the morning.

Sing as a partner song with "Sinner Man."

El Coqui

Puerto Rican Folk Song

VERSE **With a swinging motion**

El co - qui, el co - qui so en - chants me;
El co - qui, el co - qui, a mi me en - can - ta,

El co - qui sings his song all night long.
Es tan lin - do el can - tar del co - qui;

Ev - ery night when I lie on my pil - low,
Por las noch - es al ir a a - cost - ar - me,

He lulls me to sleep with his song. _____
Me a - dor - me - ce can - tan - do a si. _____

REFRAIN

Co - qui, co - qui, co - qui, qui, qui, qui.
Co - qui. co - qui, co - qui. qui, qui, qui,

Co - qui, co - qui, co - qui, qui, qui, qui.
Co - qui, co - qui, co - qui. qui, qui, qui.

Pronounce co-qui: koh key

Fill Your Pitcher

Welsh traditional tune

1. Come to the brook and fill your pitch-er, Mer-ry the wa-ter as it flows,
2. Come to the well and fill your pitch-er, Deep the wa-ter there be-low,

Hap-py and gay as life's ad-ven-ture, Where does it lead to? No man knows.
Calm and peace-ful is its jour-ney Qui-et the path it still must go.

Youth to youth is call-ing, call-ing, As__ the wa-ter rush-es on,
Age to age is call-ing, call-ing, So__ the wa-ter seem__ to cry,

Come to the brook and fill your pitch-er, Youth is the time for joy and song.
Come to the well and fill your pitch-er, Fill it be-fore the well is dry.

Five Little Chickadees

Happily

1. Five lit-tle chick-a-dees, peep-ing at the door, One flew a-way and then there were four.
2. Four lit-tle chick-a-dees, sit-ting in a tree, One flew a-way and then there were three.

REFRAIN

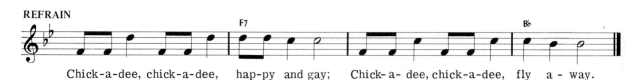

Chick-a-dee, chick-a-dee, hap-py and gay; Chick-a-dee, chick-a-dee, fly a-way.

3. Three little chickadees,
Looking at you,
One flew away
And then there were two.

4. Two little chickadees,
Sitting in the sun,
One flew away
And then there was one.

5. One little chickadee,
Left all alone,
He flew away
And then there was none.

For Health and Strength

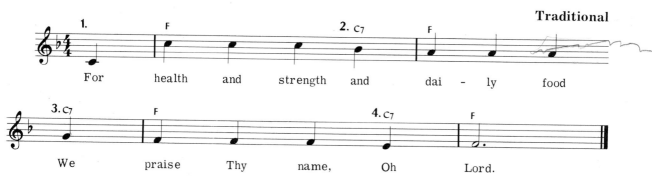

When singing in a round, play the F chord throughout.

Four in a Boat

Four in a boat and the tide rolls high, Four in a boat and the tide rolls high.

Four in a boat and the tide rolls high, Wait-ing for a pret-ty girl to come by and by.

Use the following body movement accompaniment with this song:

*Patsch means to tap thighs.

This song can be sung as a partner song with "When the Saints Go Marching In" and with the Fee, fie, fid-dle-ee-i-o section of "I've Been Workin' on the Railroad" (H.S., p. 38).

Frog's in the Meadow

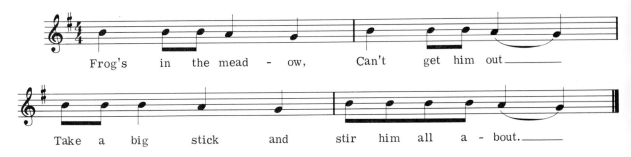

Frog's in the mead - ow, Can't get him out___

Take a big stick and stir him all a - bout.___

The melody of this song contains only three tones: B, A, and G (*Mi*, *Re*, and *Do*). Encourage children to play the song on water glasses, pop bottles, resonator bells, and piano. Sing the song using hand signals.

Gathering Nuts

Text by Patricia H. Nielsen   **Dutch Folk Tune**

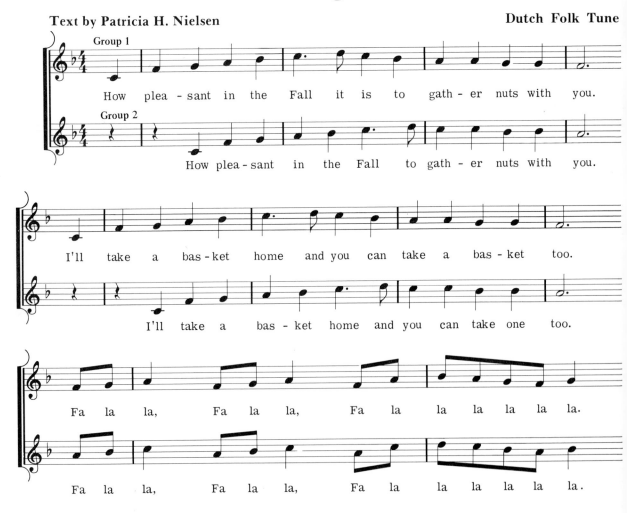

Group 1

How plea - sant in the Fall it is to gath - er nuts with you.

Group 2

How plea - sant in the Fall to gath - er nuts with you.

I'll take a bas - ket home and you can take a bas - ket too.

I'll take a bas - ket home and you can take one too.

Fa la la, Fa la la, Fa la la la la la la.

Fa la la, Fa la la, Fa la la la la la la.

Fa la la,   Fa la la,   Fa la la la la la la.

Fa la la,   Fa la la,   Fa la la la la la la.

How plea-sant in the Fall it is to gath-er nuts with you.

How plea-sant in the Fall to gath-er nuts with you.

As written this song combines polyphonic and homophonic harmony. The "A" phrases are sung as a catch (it begins as a canon, but group 2 catches up with group 1 at the end of the phrase). The "B" phrases are sung in parallel thirds, group 2 singing the melody and group 1 singing a third below.

Ginger Snap

Here   comes a pret-ty bird   through   the   win - dow

through   the   win - dow   through   the   win - dow

Here comes a pret-ty bird   through the   win - dow,   Oh   gin - ger   snap!

2. Make a little bow and tap him on the shoulders, Oh Ginger snap!

3. Take him by the shoulders and fly off to London, Oh Ginger snap!

Locate the *Do Mi Sol* pattern and hand sign or play on a melodic instrument as you sing.

Sing in partner with "Johnny, Hold Your Hand Up."

This two-chord song may be accompanied by a chant on the tone common to both the F and C chords. Ask a small group of children to sing or play on resonator bells. For example:

Pret-ty bird,   Pret-ty bird.

Going Down the Railroad

Go - ing down the rail - road, re so do. Go-ing down the rail-road, re so do.

Old_____ gon - na run all a - round. Old_____ gon - na run all a - round.

Go - ing to turn a - round. Go-ing to go back home.

After playing the game, try hand signing

Re Sol Do

Invite a child to play all the repeated tones on piano or resonator bells.

Go - ing down the

The class may enjoy hand signing and singing *"Do"* on those repeated tones. Sing in Canon. The second part may begin whenever they choose.

Going Over the Sea

1. When I was one I ate a bun, go - in' o-ver the sea.
2. When I was two I buckled my shoe, go - in' o-ver the sea.

I jumped a - board a sail - ing ship and a sail-or man said to me,
I jumped a - board a sail - ing ship and a sail-or man said to me,

Go - in' o - ver, go - in' un - der, Stand at at - ten - tion
Go - in' o - ver, go - in' un - der, Stand at at - ten - tion

like a sol - dier, With a one, two, three!
like a sol - dier, With a one, two, three!

3. When I was three, I climbed a tree, etc.

4. When I was four, I fell on the floor, etc.

5. When I was five, I took a dive, etc.

6. When I was six, I got in a fix, etc.

7. When I was sev'n, I went to heav'n, etc.

8. When I was eight, I ran out the gate, etc.

9. When I was nine, the world was mine!, etc.

10. When I was ten, now sing it again, etc.

Ground Hog

Tennessee

Sharp-en up your knife and whis-tle to your dog Sharp-en up your knife and whis-tle to your dog,

We're off to the wood to ketch a ground hog, ground___ hog

Ostinato

Whis-tle to your dog.

Divide class into 2 groups — one singing ostinato pattern, the other singing melody; both parts sing last measure in unison.

Hail to Britannia

VERSE

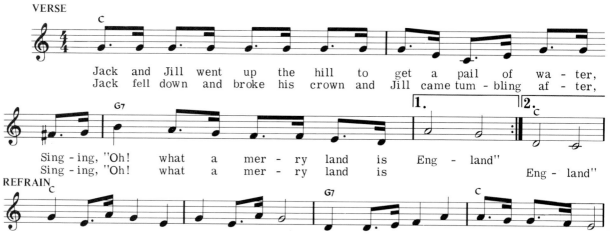

Jack and Jill went up the hill to get a pail of wa - ter,
Jack fell down and broke his crown and Jill came tum - bling af - ter,

Sing - ing, "Oh! what a mer - ry land is Eng - land"
Sing - ing, "Oh! what a mer - ry land is Eng - land"

REFRAIN

Hail to Bri-tan - nia God save the king! These times be good times else we would not sing!

Hok-ey pok-ey, pen-ny a loaf-y, Taste be-fore you buy, sing-ing, "Oh, what a mer-ry land is Eng-land.

Substitute other nursery rhymes for the verse.

Happy Is the Miller

Hap - py is the mill - er as he lives by him - self,

As the wheel turns a - round it's the get - ting of his wealth,

One hand on the hop - per and the oth - er on the sack,

As the wheel turns a - round and the mill - er cries "grab!"

Locate the ti dem rhythm pattern and encourage children to find different ways to move to that rhythm pattern when it comes in the song.

Find other songs with ti dem.

Harvest Song

Danish Song Traditional Words

Lively

1. Out in the mead - ows the grain has been cra - dled,
2. Soon we shall har - vest the corn which is ri - pened;

Rye and wheat are stacked and soon the hay is in the barn.
Let us count our bless - ings as the grain is gath - ered in

Trees have been shak - en and fruit has been gath - ered,
So in the full - ness of boun - ti - ful har - vest,

Home - ward now we wend our way up - on the fi - nal load.
Let us keep an o - pen heart for those who are in need.

REFRAIN

Glad - ness on ev - ery hand, Games and dance through - out the land;

Sing - ing mer - ri - ly we bind the hap - py har - vest wreath.

In this song, the first and third phrases of the verse outline the I chord. On these phrases, children could play the melody on the bells or sing the tone syllables using the hand signals.

He Is Born
Il est ne'

French Carol

Joyfully

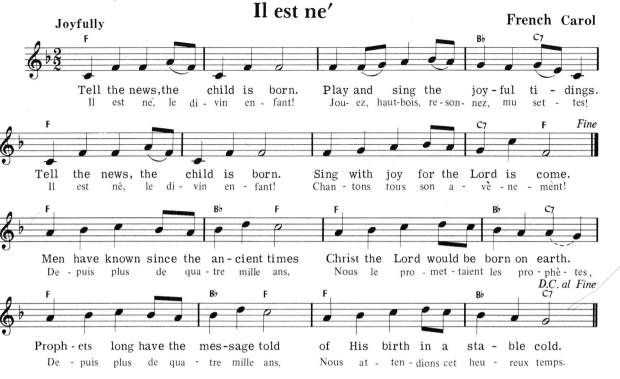

Tell the news, the child is born. Play and sing the joy-ful ti - dings.
Il est né, le di - vin en - fant! Jou - ez, haut-bois, re - son - nez, mu set - tes!

Tell the news, the child is born. Sing with joy for the Lord is come.
Il est né, le di - vin en - fant! Chan - tons tous son a - vè - ne - ment!

Men have known since the an - cient times Christ the Lord would be born on earth.
De - puis plus de qua - tre mille ans, Nous le pro - met - taient les pro - phè - tes,

D.C. al Fine

Proph - ets long have the mes-sage told of His birth in a sta - ble cold.
De - puis plus de qua - tre mille ans, Nous at - ten - dions cet heu - reux temps.

Head, Shoulders, Knees and Toes

Traditional

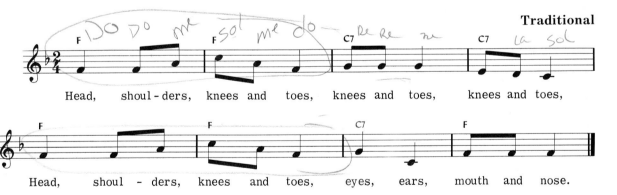

Head, shoul - ders, knees and toes, knees and toes, knees and toes,

Head, shoul - ders, knees and toes, eyes, ears, mouth and nose.

German:

Kopf, Schulter, Knie und Fuss,
Knie und Fuss, Knie und Fuss,
Kopf, Schulter, Knie und Fuss.
Aug', Ohr, Mund und Nas'.

French:

Tête, épaule, genou et pied,
Genou et pied, genou et pied,
Tête, épaule, genou et pied,
Oeil, oreille, bouche et nez.

Spanish:

Cabeza, hombro, rodilla y pie,
Rodilla y pie, rodilla y pie,
Cabeza, hombro, rodilla y pie,
Ojo, oreja, boca y nariz.

Japanese:

Atama, kata, hiza to ashi,
Hiza to ashi, hiza to ashi,
Atama, kata, hiza to ashi,
Me, mimi, kuchi to hana.

Here Comes Saint Nicholas

Excitedly

Dutch Folk Song

See there comes the steam-boat from far a-way Spain;
Zie ginds komt de stoom-boot uit Span-je weer aan,

On board is Saint Nicho-las, he's wav-ing his cane;
Hij brengt ons Sint Nik-o-laas, ik zie hem al staan,

A-stride his white horse he is pranc-ing a-round,
Hoe hup-pelt zijn paard-je het bek op-en neer!

And ev-'ry-one__ waits for this mer-ri-est sound.
Hoe waaj-en de wim-ples al heen en al weer!

2. Saint Nicholas rides through the city this day,
   Behind him his helper, he's ready, they say,
   To leave for good children a bag full of toys,
   A bundle of switches for bad girls and boys.

Hey Lolly

Hey Lol-ly Lol-ly Lol-ly,__ Hey Lol-ly Lol-ly-o __

Hey Lol-ly Lol-ly Lol-ly,__ Hey Lol-ly Lol-ly-o. __

Have the children make up their own verses to this song. Younger children can think up phrases that could be repeated in the song. (For example, "Let's all clap our hands together.") Older children might enjoy thinking of phrases that have rhyming endings. (For example, "Let's all clap our hands together . . . We'll have fun, despite the weather . . .")

Hickety Tickety Bumblebee

Hick - et - y   Tick - et - y   bum - ble - bee

Can   you   sing   your   name   to   me?

This song uses only three tones: G, A, and C (*Sol*, *La*, and *Do*). Invite children to sing the song using hand signs or play on resonator bells or piano.

Children may enjoy playing this song on black notes of piano beginning on C sharp or F sharp.

High Stepping Horses

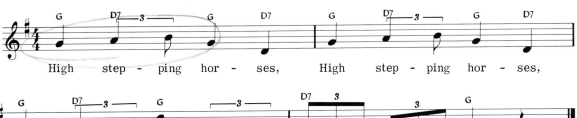

High   step - ping   hor - ses,   High   step - ping   hor - ses,

High   step - ping   hor - ses   go   jig - ge - ty jig - ge - ty jog.

Invite children to find the tri - pl - ti rhythmic pattern and play on rhythm instruments as it occurs in the song.

Hine Ma Tov (A)

Text from Psalm 133 "How good and how pleasant it is for brethren to dwell together in unity."

Smoothly, not too fast

Israeli Round

Hi - ne ma tov u - ma na - im,

she - vet a - chim gam ya - chad.

Hi - ne ma _____ tov,

she - vet a - chim gam ya - chad.

Hine Ma Tov (B)

Lively

Traditional Israeli Song

Hi - ne ma tov u - ma na - im, she - vet a - chim gam ya - chad.

Hi - ne ma tov, Hi - ne ma tov, la la la la la la la la la la.

Use tambourine, finger cymbals, and drums to enhance the character of this Israeli dance tune.

Notice that this song is really in the Dorian mode, even though it is chorded in "d" minor.

Hine Ma Tov (C)

Accented, not too fast

Traditional Yemenite Song

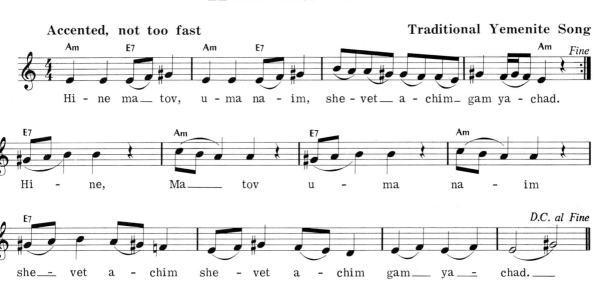

Hi - ne ma — tov, u - ma na - im, she - vet — a - chim — gam ya - chad.

Hi - ne, Ma — tov u - ma na - im

D.C. al Fine

she — vet a - chim she - vet a - chim gam — ya — chad. —

Holla Hi, Holla Ho

German Folk Song

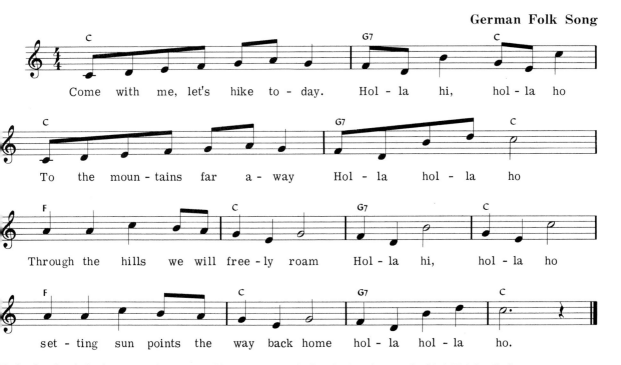

Come with me, let's hike to - day. Hol - la hi, hol - la ho

To the moun - tains far a - way Hol - la hol - la ho

Through the hills we will free - ly roam Hol - la hi, hol - la ho

set - ting sun points the way back home hol - la hol - la ho.

Notice that the pitches in measure 2 are repeated in measures 7 and 8, but the durations are doubled. This is called rhythmic augmentation. Can you find another example of augmentation?

Hop, Old Squirrel

Moderately fast

Hop, old squirrel, ei-dle-dum, ei-dle-dum, Hop old squirrel, ei-dle-dum de

Hop, old squirrel, ei-dle-dum, ei-dle-dum, Hop, old squirrel, ei-dle-dum de

Ask the children to substitute other body movements and appropriate animals.

Examples:

1. Fly little bird, eideldum, eideldum, etc.

2. Leap, old frog

3. Skip around

Have a child accompany this song on a resonator bell by playing the repeated tones (on A) each time the words "Hop old squirrel" are sung.

How Many Miles to Bethlehem?

Maine

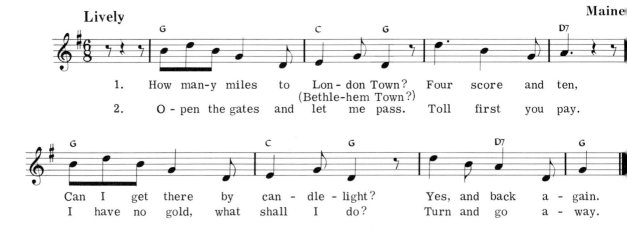

Lively

1. How man-y miles to Lon - don Town? Four score and ten,
   (Bethle-hem Town?)
2. O - pen the gates and let me pass. Toll first you pay.

Can I get there by can - dle - light? Yes, and back a - gain.
I have no gold, what shall I do? Turn and go a - way.

The Huron Carol

Huron Text by Father Jean de Brebeuf
English Translation by J. E. Middleton

1. Twas in the moon of win - ter time When all the birds had fled,

That might - y Git - chi Ma - ni - tou Sent an - gel choirs in - stead;

Be - fore their light the stars grew dim And wond-ring hunt - ers heard the hymn

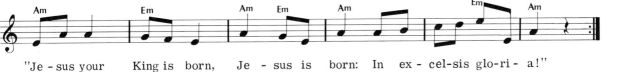

"Je - sus your King is born, Je - sus is born: In ex - cel-sis glo-ri - a!"

First Stanza in Huron
Estennialon de tsonoue
Jesous ahatonhia
Onnaouateoua d'oki
N'onouandaskouaentak
Ennochien skouatrihotat
N'onouandilonrachatha
Jesous ahatonhia.

First Stanza in French
Chrétiens, prenez courage,
Jésus Sauveur est né!
Du malin les ouvrages
Ajamais sont ruinés
Quand il chante merveille,
A ces troublants appas
Ne pretez plus l'oreille:
"Jésus est né: In excelsis gloria!"

2. Within a lodge of broken bark
   The tender Babe was found
   A ragged robe of rabbit skin
   Enwrapped His beauty 'round;
   And as the hunter braves drew nigh
   The angel song rang loud and high:
   "Jesus your King is born,
   Jesus is born: In excelsis gloria!"

3. The earliest moon of winter time
   Is not so round and fair
   As was the ring of glory on
   The helpless Infant there.
   The chiefs from far before Him knelt
   With gifts of fox and beaver pelt.
   "Jesus your King is born,
   Jesus is born: In excelsis gloria!"

4. O children of the forest free,
   O sons of Manitou,
   The Holy Child of earth and heaven
   Is born today for you.
   Come kneel before the radiant Boy
   Who brings you beauty, peace, and joy.
   "Jesus your King is born,
   Jesus is born: In excelsis gloria!"

Ifca's Castle

Czech Folk Song

VERSE

1. A - bove a plain of gold and green
2. But no 'tis not his lift - ing head,

A young boy's head is clear - ly seen.
'Tis If - ca's cas - tle spires in - stead.

REFRAIN

A - hu - ya, hu - ya, hu - ya - ya, Swift - ly flow - ing wa - ter,

A - hu - ya, hu - ya, hu - ya - ya, Swift - ly flow - ing wa - ter.

If You're Happy

Traditional

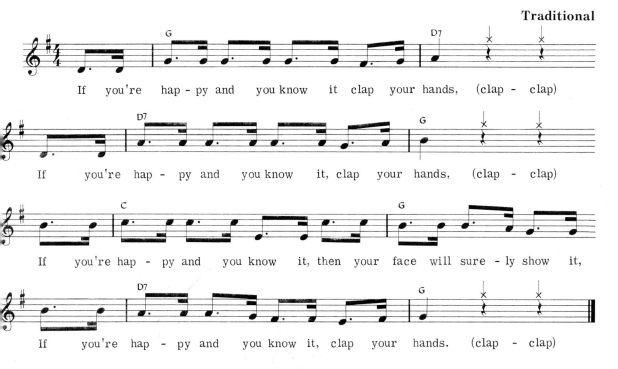

If you're hap - py and you know it clap your hands, (clap - clap)

If you're hap - py and you know it, clap your hands, (clap - clap)

If you're hap - py and you know it, then your face will sure - ly show it,

If you're hap - py and you know it, clap your hands. (clap - clap)

2. If you're happy and you know it, nod your head.

3. If you're happy and you know it, stamp your foot.

4. If you're happy and you know it, turn around.

Help the children make up additional verses to this song.

I Love the Mountains

Traditional Song

Harmony Parts:

Have part of the group repeat the first two measures of the refrain throughout the song.
Have part of the group sing or play on bells the following ostinato throughout the song.

Boom.   Boom   Boom   Boom.

I See You

I see you, I see you   Tra - la - la - la - la - la - la

I see you, I see you   Tra - la - la - la - la.

I see you and you see me and   I see you and you see me.

I Wonder as I Wander

Words and Music by
John Jacob Niles

1. I won-der as I wan-der out un-der the sky
2. When Mar-y birthed Je-sus 'twas in a cow's stall.
3. If Je-sus had want-ed for an-y wee thing,
4. I won-der as I wan-der out un-der the sky

How Je-sus our Sav-ior did come for to die
With wise men and farm-ers and shep-herds and all,
A star in the sky or a bird on the wing,
How Je-sus our Sav-ior did come for to die

For poor on'-ry peo-ple like you and like I.
But high from God's heav-en a star's light did fall,
Or all of God's an-gels in heav-en to sing,
For poor on'-ry peo-ple like you and like I.

I won-der as I wan-der out un-der the sky.
And the prom-ise of a-ges it then did re-call.
He sure-ly could have it, 'cause He was the King.
I won-der as I wan-der out un-der the sky.

I Wrote a Letter

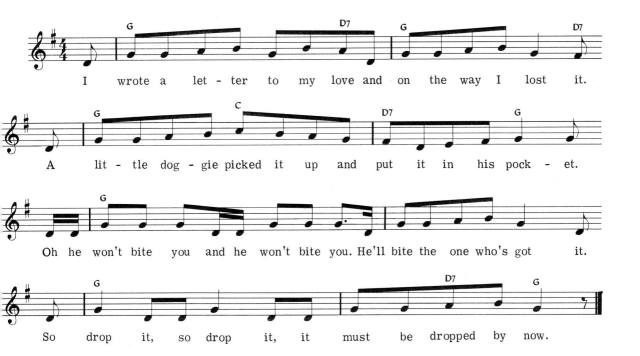

I wrote a let - ter to my love and on the way I lost it.

A lit - tle dog - gie picked it up and put it in his pock - et.

Oh he won't bite you and he won't bite you. He'll bite the one who's got it.

So drop it, so drop it, it must be dropped by now.

I've Been to Haarlem

Traditional American

I've been to Haar - lem I've been to Do - ver

I've trav - elled this wide world all ov - er

ov - er ov - er three times ov - er

Drink all the lem - on - ade and turn the glass - es ov - er.

Sail - ing east sail - ing west sail - ing ov - er the o - cean

Bet - ter watch out when the boat be - gins to rock or you'll lose your girl in the o - cean.

Use the following movement activities with this song:

Move to the underlying beat

Move to the melodic rhythm

Move to the accent (Do a Grand Right and Left on accent pattern)

Jenny Jones

1. We've come to see   Miss Jen - ny Jones, Miss Jen - ny Jones, Miss Jen - ny Jones.

We've   come   to   see   Miss Jen - ny Jones.   How   is   she   now?____

2. Miss Jenny's doing the washing — you can't see her now.

3. Miss Jenny's washing the windows — you can't see her now.

4. Miss Jenny's doing the gardening — you can't see her now.

5. Miss Jenny's doing the shopping — you can't see her now.

6. Miss Jenny Jones is ill now — you can't see her now.

7. Miss Jenny Jones is dying — you can't see her now.

8. Miss Jenny Jones is dead now — you can't see her now.

9. What color shall we bury her in — shall it be red?

10. Oh red is for firemen — that will never do.

11. What color shall we bury her in — shall it be blue?

12. Oh blue is for sailormen — that will never do.

13. What color shall we bury her in — shall it be pink?

14. Oh pink is for babies — that will never do.

15. What color shall we bury her in — shall it be black?

16. Oh black is for mourners — that will never do.

17. What color shall we bury her in — shall it be white?

18. Oh white is for dead people — that will surely do.

19. Oh where shall we bury her? — under the apple tree.

20. I dreamed I saw a ghost last night — the ghost of Jenny Jones.

Try singing this song in partner with "Three Dukes a Riding."

Jesus, the Christ, Is Born

Carol from Tennessee
Arranged by John Jacob Niles

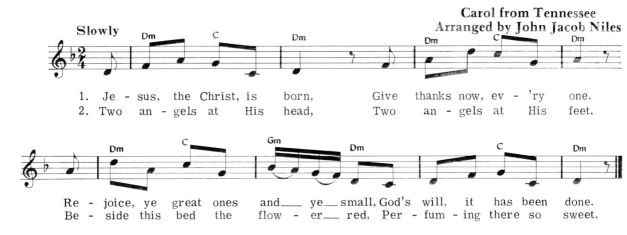

1. Je - sus, the Christ, is born, Give thanks now, ev - 'ry one.
2. Two an - gels at His head, Two an - gels at His feet.

Re - joice, ye great ones and__ ye__ small, God's will, it has been done.
Be - side this bed the flow - er__ red, Per - fum - ing there so sweet.

3. Ye mighty kings of earth, Before the manger bed,
   Cast down, cast down your golden crown From off your royal head.

4. Jesus, the Christ, is born, Give thanks now, everyone.
   Rejoice, ye great ones and ye small, God's will, it has been done.

Play this ostinato on bells or pluck autoharp strings.

Reprinted by permission of ASCAP.

Jingle at the Window

Pass one win - dow Ti - de - o Pass two win - dows Ti - de - o

Pass Three win - dows Ti - de - o Jin - gle at the win - dow Ti - de-o

Ti - de - o Ti - de - o Jin - gle at the win - dow Ti - de - o.

The John B. Sails

Folk Song From The Bahama Islands

2. The first mate he got sad, feelin' awf'ly bad, captain come aboard, took him away. Please let me alone and let me go home, well, I feel so break up, I want to go home.

3. The poor cook he got fits, and throw way all the grits, then he took and eat up all of the corn. Please let me go home, I want to go home, well, this is the worst trip since I was born.

Johnny Get Your Hair Cut

Oh John - ny   get   your   hair   cut,   hair   cut   hair   cut

John - ny   get   your   hair   cut,   just   like   me.

Help children discover the following pattern in the song and hand sign or play on resonator bells each time it occurs:

La   Sol

Johnny Has Gone for a Soldier

Slowly   American Folk Song

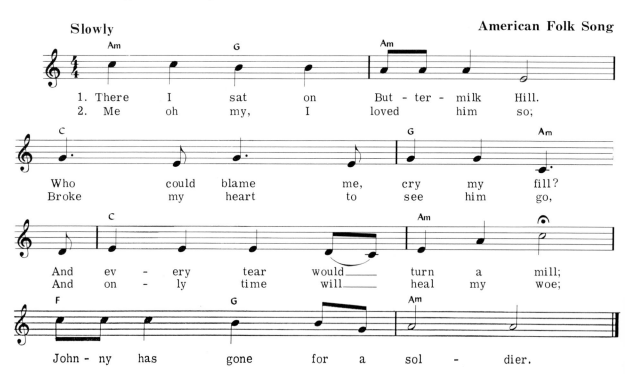

1. There   I   sat   on   But - ter - milk   Hill.
2. Me   oh   my,   I   loved   him   so;

Who   could   blame   me,   cry   my   fill?
Broke   my   heart   to   see   him   go,

And   ev - ery   tear   would____   turn   a   mill;
And   on - ly   time   will____   heal   my   woe;

John - ny   has   gone   for   a   sol - dier.

Johnny, Hold Your Hand Up!

John-ny,   hold your hand up,   hold your hand up,   hold your hand up.

John - ny   hold your hand up,   hold your hand up   to   the   sky.

ing in partner with "Ginger Snap."

Create new verses to this tune. "Mary put your head down," etc.

Kitty Kitty Casket

Kit - ty Kit -ty Cas - ket, a   green and yel - low bas - ket

I   found my hand-ker-chief yes-ter- day, It's   all full of mud so I   tossed it a-way.

Help children locate the repeated *Do* pattern in the second line of the song. Hand sign or play on resonator bells.

This song uses only four tones: D, E, G, and B. Try playing it on resonator bells.

It may also be played on the black keys of the piano by beginning on G flat.

Let Us Sing Together

Adapted From Czech Folk Tune

Let us sing to-geth-er; Let us sing to-geth-er, One and all a joy - ous song.

Let us sing to-geth - er, One and all a joy - ous song.

Let us sing a - gain and a-gain, Let us sing a - gain and a - gain,

Let us sing a - gain and a - gain, One and all a joy - ous song.

Sing as a four-part round.

Little Bird
Kommt ein Vogel geflogen

Wenzel Muller
English. text Patricia H. Nielsen

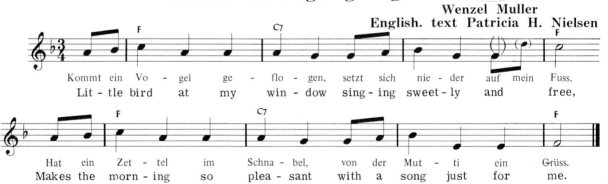

Kommt ein Vo - gel ge - flo - gen, setzt sich nie - der auf mein Fuss.
Lit - tle bird at my win - dow sing - ing sweet - ly and free,

Hat ein Zet - tel im Schna - bel, von der Mut - ti ein Grüss.
Makes the morn - ing so plea - sant with a song just for me.

Alternate English Words:

Fly away little birdie way up in the sky;
Come and tell me dear birdie who taught you to fly.

Alternate English words used by permission Richards Institute of Music Education and Research.

Little Boy

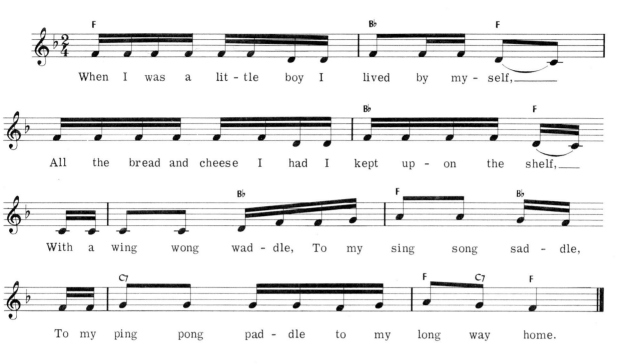

When I was a lit - tle boy I lived by my - self,____

All the bread and cheese I had I kept up - on the shelf,____

With a wing wong wad - dle, To my sing song sad - dle,

To my ping pong pad - dle to my long way home.

Little Cottage in the Wood

German Folk Tune

Lit - tle cot - tage in the wood, Lit - tle man by the win-dow stood,

Saw a rab - bit hop - ping by, knock - ing at the door.____

"Help me, help me, help me, "he said, "Or, the hun - ter will shoot me dead!"

"Come, lit - tle rab - bit, come with me, Hap - py we will be."____

Have the children create actions to this song. After they have sung it several times, have them sing parts of the song "inside" while continuing to do the actions. Progressively sing more parts "inside" until the children can do the whole song that way, doing only the actions on the "outside."

Little Johnny England

Use the following movement activity with this song:

1. Divide into two circles, one inner, one outer

2. Move in opposite directions for first four lines: stop on *Mi Re Do* cadence

3. Fifth and Sixth lines: Patschen (tap legs) four times; clap four times; snap four times; clap twice

4. Seventh and Eighth lines: R elbows touch; L elbows touch (do pattern three times); stomp feet on last measure

5. Repeat game and find a new partner

Little Wheel

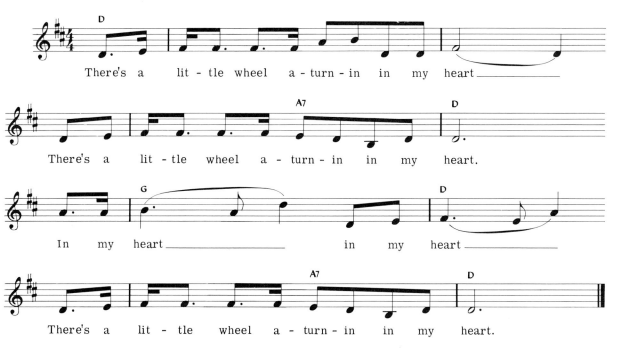

There's a   lit – tle wheel   a – turn – in   in   my   heart_____

There's a   lit – tle   wheel   a – turn – in   in   my   heart.

In   my   heart _____   in   my   heart _____

There's a   lit – tle   wheel   a – turn – in   in   my   heart.

2. There's a little song a singin' . . .

3. There's a little smile a-smiling . . .

Make up own verses

This song is based on the pentatonic scale D E F♯ A B. Any of these tones may be combined into a simple 2, 3, or 4 note ostinato to sing or play as an accompaniment.

Voice, bells, or piano

Lit – tle Wheel   Lit-tle Wheel

Play on bells or pluck on autoharp

Maori Stick Song

Au - e, au - e ____ ka - ma - te au. E hi - ne ho - ki 'ho - ra. ____

E - pa - pa wai-a - ri ta-ku nei ma - hi ta-ku nei ma - hi tu - ku roi ma(ta). Au

This song (text) seems to be a lament of Rangi (Heaven) for Papa (Earth) begging her to return to him. This would have evolved from ancient Polynesian legend concerning the creation in which Rangi is considered the Sky Father and Papa, the Earth Mother.

Directions for using sticks:

Chorus: Tap floor, tap sticks, circle both hands away from each other (repeat) (on "hora" tap floor, tap sticks twice, tap floor)

Verse 1: floor, sticks, throw right (to partner); floor, sticks, throw left (repeat)

Verse 2: floor, sticks, throw both sticks (one pair inside, one pair outside) (repeat)

Verse 3: floor, sticks, throw right, throw left, throw right, throw left (repeat)

Verse 4: throw right, throw left (repeat)

Verse 5: (by self) floor, sticks, tap tips of sticks to right, then flip sticks (repeat to left)

Verse 6: floor, sticks, tap, flip, throw right, throw left

Maple Swamp

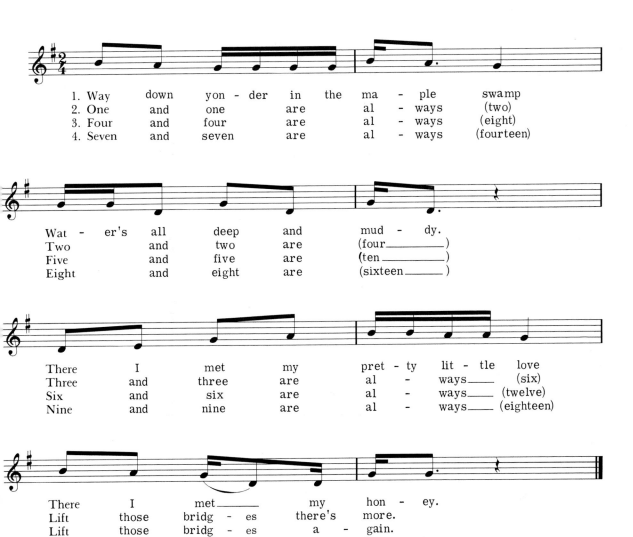

1. Way down yon - der in the ma - ple swamp
2. One and one are al - ways (two)
3. Four and four are al - ways (eight)
4. Seven and seven are al - ways (fourteen)

Wat - er's all deep and mud - dy.
Two and two are (four_____)
Five and five are (ten_____)
Eight and eight are (sixteen_____)

There I met my pret - ty lit - tle love
Three and three are al - ways_____ (six)
Six and six are al - ways_____ (twelve)
Nine and nine are al - ways_____ (eighteen)

There I met_____ my hon - ey.
Lift those bridg - es there's more.
Lift those bridg - es a - gain.
Ten and ten_____ are twen - ty.

This song is based on the pentatonic scale G A B D E. Any of these tones may be combined into a simple ostinato to sing or play as an accompaniment.

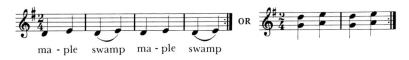

ma - ple swamp ma - ple swamp

Show the class a chart with ti dem and demonstrate its sound. Help them to sing the ti dem in the song and clap each time the pattern occurs.

Find other songs with ti dem.

Mary Had a Baby

Tenderly

Spiritual

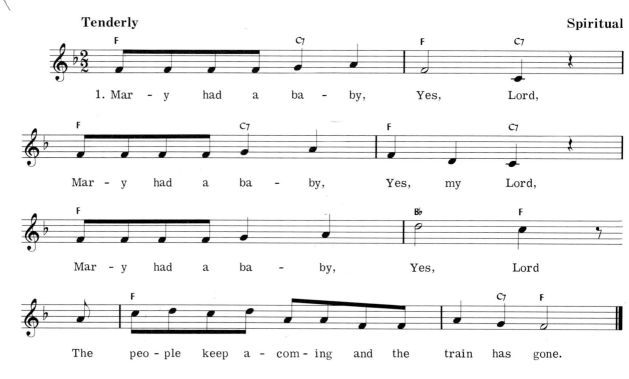

1. Mar - y had a ba - by, Yes, Lord,

Mar - y had a ba - by, Yes, my Lord,

Mar - y had a ba - by, Yes, Lord

The peo - ple keep a - com - ing and the train has gone.

2. What did Mary name him . . .

3. Mary named him Jesus . . .

4. Where was Jesus born . . .

5. Born in lowly stable . . .

6. Where did Mary lay him . . .

7. Laid him in a manger . . .

Mary Wore a Red Dress

Virginia

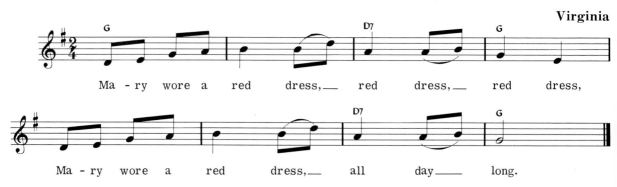

Ma - ry wore a red dress, __ red dress, __ red dress,

Ma - ry wore a red dress, __ all day __ long.

"Mary Wore a Red Dress" is based on the pentatonic scale G A B D E. Combine any of these tones to create a simple melodic or chordal ostinato.

All day long   All day long   OR

Substitute children's names as well as clothes they are wearing. Ask the children to decide how fast or slow, loud or soft the song should be.

Michael Finnigin

Lively   Traditional

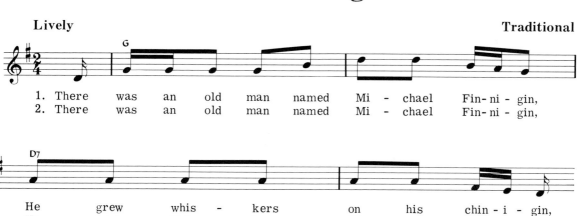

1. There was an old man named Mi - chael Fin - ni - gin,
2. There was an old man named Mi - chael Fin - ni - gin,

He grew whis - kers on his chin - i - gin,
He went fish - ing with a pin - i - gin,

The wind blew them off but they grew in - i - gin,
caught a fish but dropped it in - i - gin,

poor old Mi - chael Fin - ni - gin. Be - gin - i - gin!
poor old Mi - chael Fin - ni - gin. Be - gin - i - gin!

3. There was an old man named Michael Finnigin,
Climbed a tree and barked his shinigin,
He took off many years of skinigin,
Poor old Michael Finnigin! Beginigin!

4. There was an old man named Michael Finnigin,
He grew fat and then grew thinigin,
He died and then he had to beginigin,
Poor old Michael Finnigin. It's the endigin!

Mistress More

Jovially

Traditional Irish Game Song

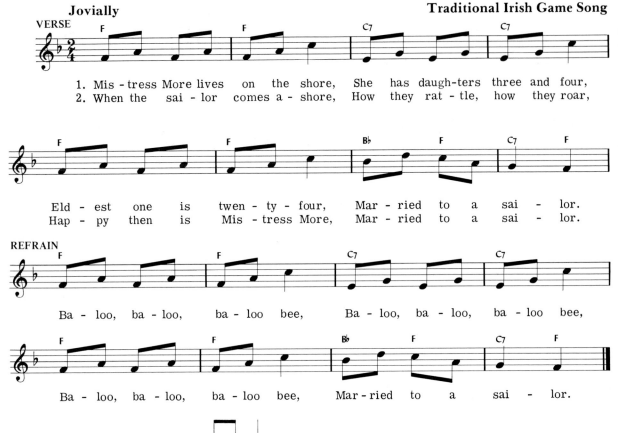

VERSE

1. Mis - tress More lives on the shore, She has daugh-ters three and four,
2. When the sai - lor comes a - shore, How they rat - tle, how they roar,

Eld - est one is twen - ty - four, Mar - ried to a sai - lor.
Hap - py then is Mis - tress More, Mar - ried to a sai - lor.

REFRAIN

Ba - loo, ba - loo, ba - loo bee, Ba - loo, ba - loo, ba - loo bee,

Ba - loo, ba - loo, ba - loo bee, Mar - ried to a sai - lor.

The children will find the rhythm pattern ti ti ta six times in the song. They may clap it or play it on a rhythm instrument.

The Moon Is Coming Out

Serenely

Japanese Children's Song

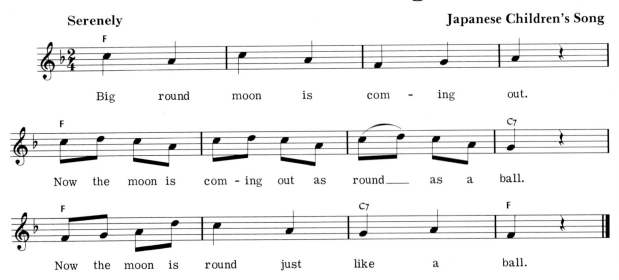

Big round moon is com - ing out.

Now the moon is com - ing out as round___ as a ball.

Now the moon is round just like a ball.

This song is based on the pentatonic scale F G A C D. Any of these tones may be combined into a simple 2, 3, or 4 note ostinato to play as an accompaniment.
This song may be played on the black notes of the piano beginning on C sharp.

Music in the Air

Words and Music by George Root

Smoothly

There's mu - sic in the air,_____ When the in - fant morn is nigh.

There's mu - sic in the air,_____ When the in - fant morn is nigh.

And faint its blush is seen _____ On the bright and laugh-ing sky.

And faint its blush is seen _____ On the bright and laugh-ing sky.

Man - y a harp's ec - stat - ic sound Thrills us with a joy pro-found,

Man - y a harp's ec - stat - ic sound Thrills us with a joy pro-found,

While we list en - chant - ed there To the mu - sic in the air.

While we list en - chant - ed there To the mu - sic in the air.

Navajo Happy Song

Navajo Indian Song

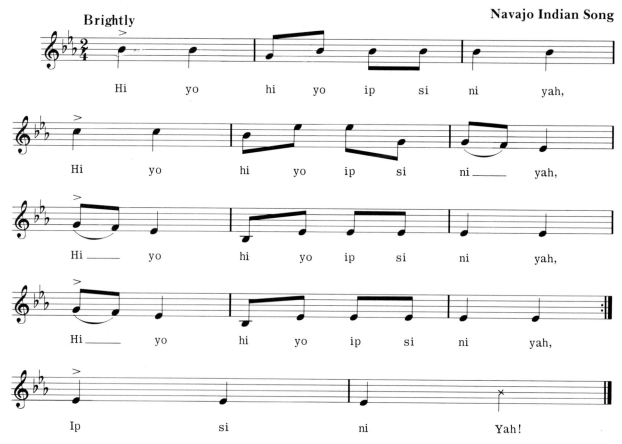

Brightly

Hi yo hi yo ip si ni yah,

Hi yo hi yo ip si ni _____ yah,

Hi _____ yo hi yo ip si ni yah,

Hi _____ yo hi yo ip si ni yah,

Ip si ni Yah!

The "Navajo Happy Song" is based on the pentatonic scale E♭ F G B♭ C. Create simple ostinato patterns by combining any of the tones.

Try playing rhythmic ostinati such as:

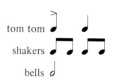

tom tom

shakers

bells

The Noble Duke of York

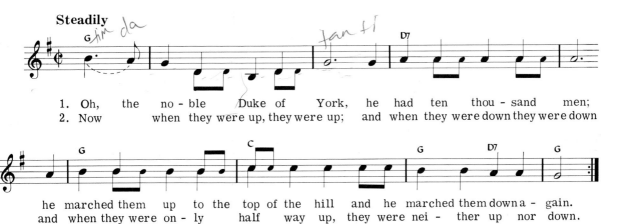

1. Oh, the no - ble Duke of York, he had ten thou - sand men;
2. Now when they were up, they were up; and when they were down they were down

he marched them up to the top of the hill and he marched them down a - gain.
and when they were on - ly half way up, they were nei - ther up nor down.

Alternate words:

Oh! A-hunting we will go,
A-hunting we will go;
We'll catch a fox and put him in a box,
And then we'll let him go.

Play the *Mi Re Do* pattern (B A G) on a melody instrument. Use hand signs.

Oh When the Saints

Oh when the Saints ___ go march-ing in ___ oh when the Saints go march-ing in ___

oh Lord I want to be in that num-ber When the Saints go march-ing in. ___

While one group holds the sustained notes, another may improvise an echo.

This song may be sung as a partner song with "Four in a Boar" or the fee fie fid-dle-ee-i-o section of "I've Been Working on the Railroad" (H.S., p. 38) if all are sung in the same key.

This song uses only the first five tones of the diatonic scale and may be played on tone bells, water glasses, or pop bottles.

Clap on off beats.

Old Grumbler

1. Old Grum-bler was dead and lay un-der the ground, un-der the ground, un-der the ground

Old Grum-bler was dead and lay un-der the ground, way high up.

Verse 2. "Three apple trees grew right over his head . . ."
Verse 3. "The apples were ripe and were ready to drop . . ."
Verse 4. "There came an old north wind a' blowin them off . . ."
Verse 5. "There came an old lady a-picking them up . . ."
Verse 6. "Old Grumbler jumped up and he gave her a knock . . ."
Verse 7. "Which made the old lady go hippety hop . . ."
Verse 8. "Old Grumbler lay down with a smile on his face . . ."
Verse 9. "If you want any more you can sing it yourself."

Old John Braddledum

Num - ber one num - ber one Now my song has just be - gun

with a Rum-tum tadd- le-tum Old John Bradd-le-dum Hey! what count - ry folk we be!

Number two . . . Don't like boots but I'll take a shoe
Number three . . . I like you and you like me
Number four . . . Bring some honey and then bring more
Number five . . . Food and drink keep us all alive
Number six . . . Fires are made from some dry old sticks
Number seven . . . My best friend is a boy named Kevin
Number eight . . . Swing around on the garden gate
Number nine . . . Sing with me 'cause we sound so fine
Number ten . . . Brown bears live in a great big den
Number eleven . . . Just the same as number seven
Number twelve . . . If you want anymore you can sing it yourself

Old Ship of Zion

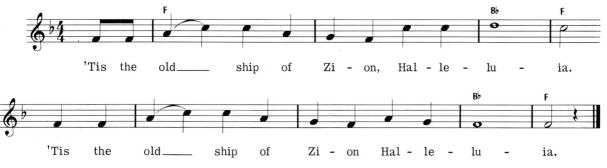

'Tis the old___ ship of Zi - on, Hal - le - lu - ia.

'Tis the old___ ship of Zi - on Hal - le - lu - ia.

Create an Orff body accompaniment such as:

Play or sing an ostinato accompaniment on the chant tone F. For example:

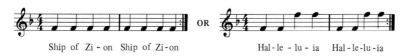

Ship of Zi - on Ship of Zi - on   OR   Hal - le - lu - ia Hal - le - lu - ia

Olive Trees Are Standing

Traditional Jewish Song
English text P. H. Nielsen

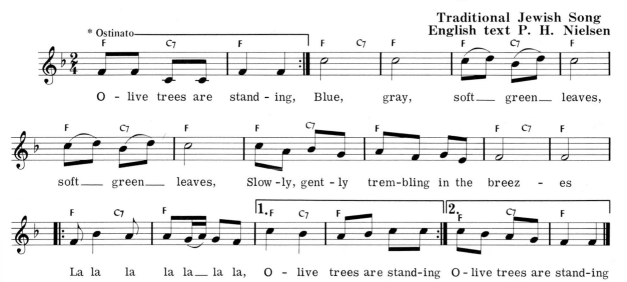

O - live trees are stand - ing, Blue, gray, soft___ green___ leaves,

soft___ green___ leaves, Slow - ly, gent - ly trem - bling in the breez - es

La la la la la___ la la, O - live trees are stand-ing O - live trees are stand-ing

*Ostinato may be used as an introduction, accompaniment, and coda.

Because the chords are the same for each two-measure pattern, the song may be sung as a 2, 3, or 4-part canon with each new group beginning after the previous group has sung the ostinato two times. Each group may either stop when reaching the end of the song or keep repeating the two-measure ostinato pattern until all groups have reached the end.

Over the Meadows

March tempo

Czech Folk Song

VERSE

O - ver the mead-ows green and wide, Bloom-ing in the sun-light. Bloom-ing in the sun-light

O - ver the mead-ows green and wide, Off we go a - roam-ing side by side. Hey!

REFRAIN

Stream-lets down moun-tain go; Pure from the win-ter snow; Join-ing, they swift-ly go;

Sing - ing of life so free.____ Call - ing to me.

Accompany this song on the Autoharp. For variety, use resonator bells as chord tones.

Penny Song

There's a pen - ny in my hand. It will trav - el through the land.____

Is it here? It is there? It will trav - el ev - 'ry where.

We are read - y you may come and find the pen - ny if you can.

"____, do you have my pen - ny?" No I don't have your pen - ny!
Yes I do have your pen - ny!

After playing the game, try hand signing or playing on resonator bells the *Sol, La, Do* pattern.

Sol,   La,   Do

Make a chart of the ti dem rhythm. Show it to the class and help them discover the rhythmic pattern each time it occurs.

Encourage children to find a way to move to the ti dem rhythm and to find the same rhythm in other songs. Create a rhythmic composition using ti dem ti ti ta.

Sing as a partner song with "Circle Left."

Pick a Bale O'Cotton

With spirit   **Southern Folk Tune**

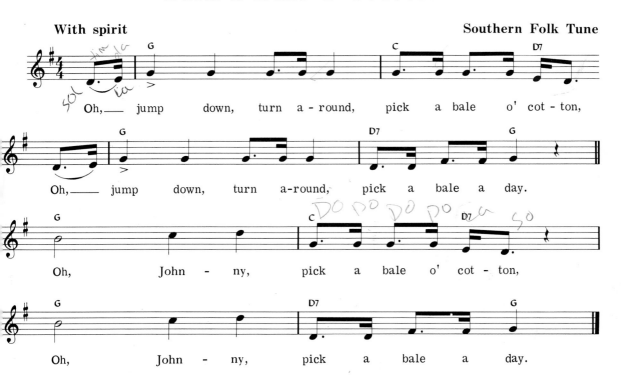

The *Sol, La, Do* pattern at the beginning of lines one and two may be played on resonator bells. You may also use hand signs for this pattern.

Try creating a dance while singing this song.

Polly Put the Kettle On

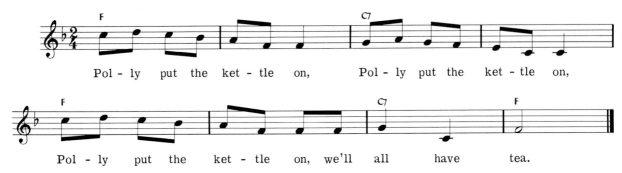

Pol - ly   put the ket - tle   on,   Pol - ly put the   ket - tle   on,

Pol - ly   put the   ket - tle   on, we'll all   have   tea.

This song may be sung as a partner song with "Bluebird," "He's Got the Whole World in His Hands" (H.S., p. 206), "Rocka My Soul," "Sandy Land" (H.S., p. 107), "Skip to My Lou" (H.S., p. 232), "Ten Little Indians" (H.S., p. 163), and "Where Oh Where is Pretty Little Susie?"

Poor Tom

Have you seen the   ghost of Tom?   Long white bones with the skin   all   gone,____

Ooh _____ oo   wouldn't it be chil - ly with   no skin   on!

Punchinello

Brightly

American, traditional

What can you do, Pun - chi - nel - lo, fun - ny fel - low?

What can you do, Pun - chi - nel - lo, fun - ny you?

2. We can do it too, Punchinello, funny fellow!
   We can do it too, Punchinello, funny you!

3. You choose one of us, Punchinello, funny fellow!
   You choose one of us, Punchinello, funny you!

One child stands in the center of a circle and makes up motions for the other children to copy.

Rain Rain
A Riddle

Rain rain the wind does blow, Stars are shin - ing to and fro.

Ma - rie Rich-ard-son says she'll die if she don't find a fel-low with a ro-guish eye.

Hand sign the following pattern with a partner as you sing the song.

Sol Do Sol Do

Find a way to move to the ti dem rhythm at the end of the song.

Find the ti dem pattern in "Circle Left," "Maple Swamp," "Penny Song," or "Rain Rain."

Riding in the Buggy, Miss Mary Jane

Moderately fast

South Carolina

Rid-ing in the bug-gy, Miss Ma-ry Jane, Miss Ma-ry Jane, Miss Ma-ry Jane,

Rid-ing in the bug-gy, Miss Ma-ry Jane, I'm a long ways from home.

REFRAIN

Who moans for me? Who moans for me?

Who moans for me, my dar-ling, Who moans for me?

Use hand signs on the *Do, Re, Mi* patterns and play the *Do, Mi, Sol* pattern on the resonator bells as you sing the song.

Rise Up, O Flame

Smoothly

Christoph Praetorius

Rise up, O flame, _____ By ___ thy ___ light glow - ing,

Show to us beau - ty, ___ Vi - sion ___ and joy.

Sing a cappella as a canon.

This is a fine example of minor scale melodic movement.

- 70 -

Rocka My Soul

Black Spiritual

Oh a rock-a my soul, in the bo-som of A-bra-ham,

Rock-a my soul in the bo-som of A-bra-ham;

Rock-a my soul in the bo-som of A-bra-ham; Oh rock-a my soul.

So high you can't get o-ver it; So low, you can't get un-der it;

So wide you can't get a-round it; You must go in at the door.

This song may be sung as a partner song with "Bluebird," "He's Got the Whole World in His Hands" (H.S., p. 206), "Polly Put the Kettle On," "Sandy Land" (H.S., p. 107), "Skip to My Lou" (H.S., p. 232), "Ten Little Indians" (H.S., p. 163), and "Where Oh Where is Pretty Little Susie?"

Roly Poly

Oh_____ Ro-ly po-ly pick-et-y pat, go see who you can see!

Oh_____ Ro-ly po-ly pick-et-y pat, and now come back to me!

Rooster Is Dead
Der Hahn ist tot

German round

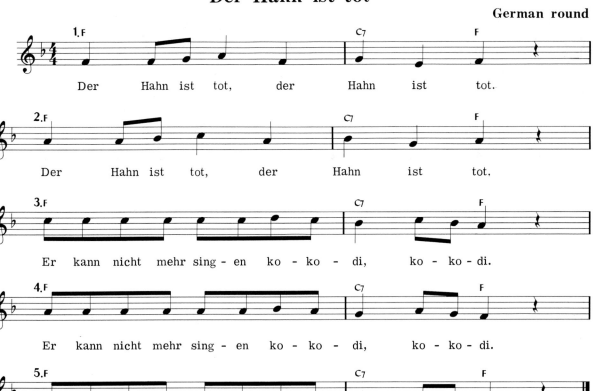

1. Der Hahn ist tot, der Hahn ist tot.

2. Der Hahn ist tot, der Hahn ist tot.

3. Er kann nicht mehr sing-en ko-ko-di, ko-ko-di.

4. Er kann nicht mehr sing-en ko-ko-di, ko-ko-di.

5. ko-ko, ko-ko, ko-ko, ko-ko-di, ko-ko-di.

English:

Rooster is dead, poor bird is dead.
Rooster is dead, poor bird is dead.
He no longer sings ko-ko-di, ko-ko-di.
He no longer sings ko-ko-di, ko-ko-di.
Ko-ko, ko-ko, ko-ko, ko-ko-di, ko-ko-di.

Alternate English words:

Let's catch a rooster, Yes let's do.
Let's catch a rooster, Yes let's do.
He'll no longer sing cookeree, cookaroo.
He'll no longer sing cookeree, cookaroo.
Coo, coo, coo, coo, coo, coo, cookeree, cookaroo.

Sally Go Round the Sun

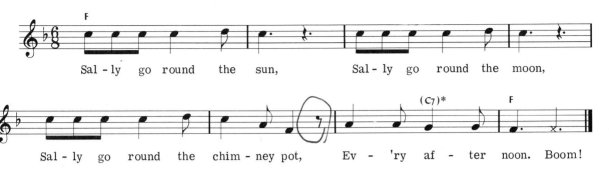

Sal - ly go round the sun, Sal - ly go round the moon,

Sal - ly go round the chim - ney pot, Ev - 'ry af - ter noon. Boom!

"Sally Go Round the Sun" is based on the pentatonic scale F G A C D. Try combining some of the tones into vocal ostinati. For example:

Sal - ly go round af - ter - noon

Invite children to sing with hand signs or play on resonator bells the following pattern as it occurs in the song:

Sol Sol Sol Sol La Sol

*this can be played as a one-chord song

- 73 -

Sambalele

Brazilian Folk Song

Poor Sam- ba - le - le they call him. Al - ways you hear his loud sigh - ing.

Ma - ny the woes that be - fall him. If you be - lieve all his cry - ing.

Sam-ba, sam- ba, sam-ba - le - le - le Throw off your cares and your mood mel- an -cho- lic.

Sam- ba, sam-ba, sam - ba - le - le - le Come out and join us in car - ni - val fro - lic.

"Sambalele" is a popular Brazilian folk song sung during their Carnival or Mardi Gras celebration.

Let the children create some other verses about the many ills of poor Sambalele.

Try singing the verse with the refrain as partner songs. Notice the sequence in phrases one and two.

Schnitzelbank

German Folk Song

1. Ist das nicht ein Schnit-zel-bank?* Ja, das ist ein Schnit-zel-bank.

Ist das nicht ein Kurz und Lang? Ja, das ist ein Kurz und Lang.

Kurz und Lang,
Schnit - zel - bank   Oh

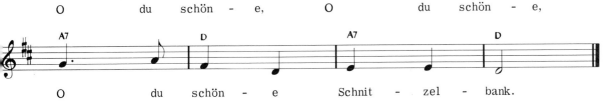

O   du   schön - e,   O   du   schön - e,

O   du   schön - e   Schnit - zel - bank.

2. Ist das nicht ein Kreuz und Quer?   Ja, das ist ein Kreuz und Quer.
   Ist das nicht ein Schiessgewehr?   Ja, das ist ein Schiessgewehr.

   Schiessgewehr, Kreuz und Quer, Kurz und Lang, Schnitzelbank, O_____

3. Langer Mann   Tannenbaum

4. Hochzeitsring   Gefährliches Ding

The song is performed by two groups — one to ask the question and one to sing the answer. Both groups sing together the cumulative section and the refrain.

Let the question group create hand motions for each item named and the answer group repeat the hand motions back.

*A Schnitzelbank is a cutting bench.
Kurz und Lang means short and long
Kreuz und Quer means criss cross
Schiessgewehr is a shotgun
Langer Mann is a very tall man
Tannenbaum is a Christmas tree
Hochzeitsring is a wedding ring
Gefährliches Ding is a horrible thing or a monster.

Verses may be created in English by finding rhyming words to end the couplets:

Is that not a _____ , Yes that is a _____

Is that not a _____ , Yes, that is a _____

_____ , _____ Oh you lovely, Oh you lovely, Oh you lovely cutting bench.

*This measure is to be repeated as many times as necessary to list the words in each verse in a cumulative style in reverse order.

Scotland's Burning

This song works nicely with hand signals.

Let children create actions for each phrase and then perform as a movement round as well as a vocal round.

Sing Your Way Home

Arr. Patricia Nielsen

Sing your way home the close of the

Sing your way home at the close of the day,

day. Sing your way home drive the shad-ows a - way.

Sing your way home drive the shad-ows a - way smile ev - 'ry

Smile ev - 'ry mile for wher - ev - er you roam it will

mile for wher - ev - er you roam, It will bright - en your

bright-en your road, It will light - en your load go - ing home.

road, It will light - en your load, If you sing your way home.

Notice the sequence in the last six measures (including pick-up).

Sinner Man

English Folk Song
Appalachian Mountain Variant

O sin-ner man, where are you going to run to?

O sin-ner man, where are you going to run to?

O sin-ner man, where are you going to run to All___ on that day?

Run to the sun: O sun, won't you hide me? Run to the sun: O sun, won't you hide me?

Run to the sun: O sun, won't you hide me? All___ on that day?

The Lord said: O sin-ner man, the sun-'ll be a-burn-ing.

The Lord said: O sin-ner man, the sun-'ll be a-burn-ing.

The Lord said: O sin-ner man, the sun-'ll be a-burn-ing All___ on that day.

Although this song is chorded in D minor, it is sung in the Dorian Mode because there is no B flat.

This is an eight-bar melody repeated three times with rhythmic variations each time.

"Sinner Man" can be sung as a partner song with the "Drunken Sailor."

Six Little Ducks

Rhythmically

American Folk Song

1. Six lit-tle ducks that I once knew, Fat ones, skin-ny ones, fair ones too,

But the one lit-tle duck with the feath-er in his back, He ruled the oth-ers with a quack, quack, quack,

quack, quack, quack, quack, quack, quack, He ruled the oth-ers with a quack, quack, quack.

2. Down to the river they would go,
   Wibble wobble, wibble wobble,
   ho-hum-ho,

3. Home from the river they would come,
   Wibble wobble, wibble wobble,
   ho-hum-hum,

The children can dramatize the song with hand motions. Experiment with different rhythm instruments on the words "quack, quack, quack." Practice inner hearing by singing the quacks silently while the instrument is playing.

Skin and Bones

Rhythmically

1. There was an old wo-man all skin and bones. Oo - oo - oo - oo.

2. One night she thought
   She'd take a walk --
   Oo-oo-oooh!
   She walked down by
   The old graveyard --
   Oo-oo-oooh!

3. She saw the bones
   A-layin' around --
   Oo-oo-oooh!
   She thought she'd sweep
   The old church-house --
   Oo-oo-oooh!

4. She went to the closet
   To get her a broom --
   Oo-oo-oooh!
   She opened the door
   And
   BOO!

Let children choose instruments to play on the rest at the end of each verse.

Sweet Nightingale
Lieb Nachtigall

German Folk Song
English text P. H. Nielsen

Tallis Canon

Thomas Ken, 1695 Thomas Tallis, 1565

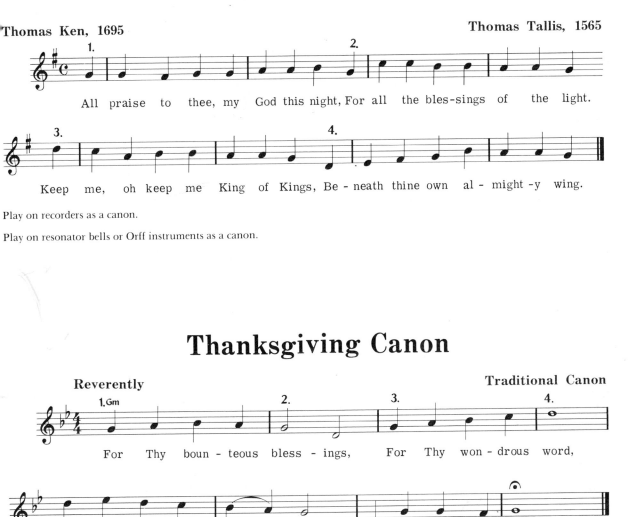

All praise to thee, my God this night, For all the bles-sings of the light.

Keep me, oh keep me King of Kings, Be - neath thine own al - might -y wing.

Play on recorders as a canon.

Play on resonator bells or Orff instruments as a canon.

Thanksgiving Canon

Reverently   Traditional Canon

For Thy boun - teous bless - ings, For Thy won - drous word,

For Thy lov - ing kind - ness We give thanks, Oh Lord.

This Old Hammer

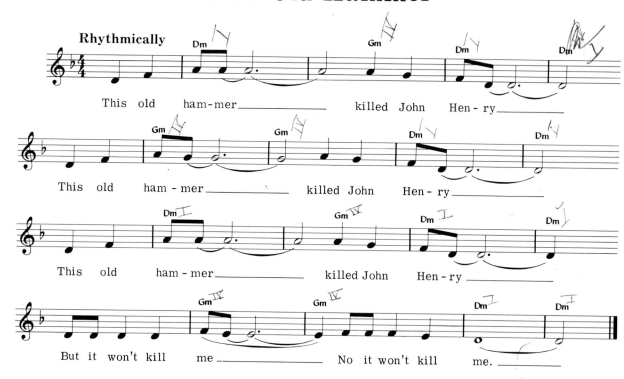

Rhythmically

This old ham-mer_____ killed John Hen-ry_____

This old ham-mer_____ killed John Hen-ry_____

This old ham-mer_____ killed John Hen-ry_____

But it won't kill me _____ No it won't kill me. _____

2. This old hammer, shines like silver (three times)
   But it rings like gold, yes, it rings like gold.

3. Take this hammer, to the walking boss (three times)
   Tell him I'm gone, yes, tell him I'm gone.

4. If he asks you, any questions (three times)
   Tell him you don't know, tell him you don't know.

This may be sung as an echo song with a second group repeating each phrase as the first group sustains the end of each phrase.

Because this is a two-chord song, a chant may be sung as an accompaniment in the tone D which is common to both chords.

This old ham-mer_ This old ham-mer_

Three Dukes A-Riding

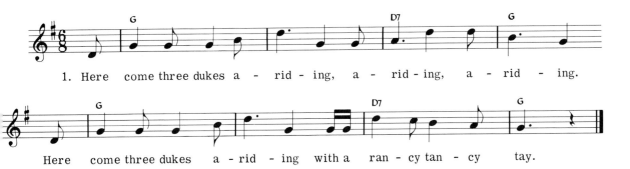

1. Here come three dukes a - rid - ing, a - rid - ing, a - rid - ing.

Here come three dukes a - rid - ing with a ran - cy tan - cy tay.

2. Oh what is your good will, Sirs, with a rancy tancy tay.

3. Oh our good will is to marry, with a rancy tancy tay.

4. Well marry one of us, Sirs, with a rancy tancy tay.

5. You're all too grubby and dirty, with a rancy tancy tay.

6. We're just as good as you, Sirs, with a rancy tancy tay.

7. You're all as stiff as pokers, with a rancy tancy tay.

8. We can bend as well as you, Sirs, with a rancy tancy tay.

VERSE 9. Through the kitch-en and through the hall, I choose the fair-est one of all

The fair - est one that I _can see is this one here who's smil-ing at me

Try singing as a partner song with "Jenny Jones."

*Toraji

Words by P. H. Nielsen
Korean Folk Tune

Toraji ten-der flow'r, bathed in the sun-set glow,

Gen-tle winds are pass-ing through the gar-den Soft pe-tals blow.

Eh - hey___ ya, eh hey___ ya, eh hey ya.

*The *toraji* is a white bell-shaped flower.

Toraji is based on the pentatonic scale F G A C D. Any of these tones may be combined into a simple 2, 3, or 4 note ostinato to sing or play as an accompaniment.

To - ra - ji   To - ra - ji   OR

Voice, bells, or piano   Bells or pluck on Autoharp

NOTE: When using a pentatonic accompaniment, do not use Autoharp chords.

Trot, Trot, Trot

Folk Song

Trot,   trot,   trot!   Trot, my po - ny,   trot!

Where it's smooth and   where it's ston-y,   Trot a-long, my   lit - tle   po - ny.

Go and nev - er   stop,   Trot, my po - ny   trot!

Encourage children to use hand signs or resonator bells on any of the following patterns as they occur in the song.

Do Mi Sol   Do Re Mi Fa Sol   Sol Fa Mi Re Do

Tzena, Tzena

Israeli Folk Song

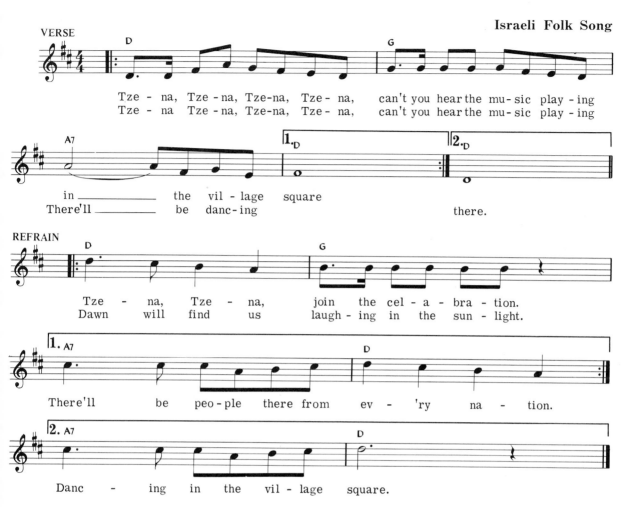

VERSE

Tze - na, Tze - na, Tze - na, Tze - na,   can't you hear the mu - sic play - ing
Tze - na Tze - na, Tze - na, Tze - na,   can't you hear the mu - sic play - ing

in _____ the vil - lage square
There'll _____ be danc - ing   there.

REFRAIN

Tze - na, Tze - na,   join the cel - a - bra - tion.
Dawn will find us   laugh - ing in the sun - light.

There'll   be peo - ple there from ev - 'ry na - tion.

Danc - ing in the vil - lage square.

The verse and the refrain of this song may be sung together as partner songs.

The Upward Trail

Traditional

We're on the up - ward trail, we're on the up - ward trail,

Sing - ing, sing - ing, ev - ery-bod-y sing - ing, as we go.

We're on the up - ward trail, we're on the up - ward trail,

Sing - ing, sing - ing, ev - ery-bod-y sing - ing, home - ward bound.

When singing as a canon, leave out chords.

The Valley Is Ringing
Es tönen die Lieder

German Round
English Text by P. H. Nielsen

1.
Es tö - nen die Lie - der, der Früh - ling kehrt wie - der,
The val - ley is ring - ing With Spring-time's sweet sing - ing.

2.
es spie - let __ der __ Hir - te auf sei - ner __ Schal - mei;*
The shep - herd __ is __ play - ing, up - on his __ Schal - mei;

3.
La la la la al la la la, _____ la la la al la la la la
La la la la la la la la, _____ la la la la la la la.

*Schal-mei — a reed pipe

Vreneli

VERSE

"O Vren - ne - li, my pret - ty one, Pray tell me where's your home."

"My home, it is in Swit - zer-land, It's made of wood and stone;

REFRAIN

stone." Yo, ho, ho, Tra, la, la, la, Yo, ho, ho, Tra la, la, la; Yo, ho

ho, Tra la la la; Yo, ho, ho, Tra, la, la, la, Yo, ho, ho, Tra, la, la, la;

Yo, ho, ho, Tra la la la; Yo, ho, ho, Tra, la, la, la; Yo, ho, ho.

Notice the octave skip between the end of the verse and the beginning of the refrain.

Wassail Song

Old English Carol

1. Here we come a - was - sail-ing a - mong the leaves so green;

Here we come a wan - d'ring, so fair to be seen;

Love and joy come to you, and to you glad Christ-mas too;

And God bless you and send you a hap - py New Year,

And God send you a hap - py New Year.

2. We are not daily beggars that beg from door to door;
But we are neighbors' children whom you have seen before.
Love and joy come to you, and to you glad Christmas too;
And God bless you and send you a happy New Year,
And God send you a happy New Year.

3. Good master and mistress, as you sit by the fire;
Pray think of us poor children who wander in the mire.
Love and joy come to you, and to you glad Christmas too;
And God bless you and send you a happy New Year,
And God send you a happy New Year.

4. God bless the master of this house, likewise the mistress too,
And all the little children that round the table go.
Love and joy come to you, and to you glad Christmas too;
And God bless you and send you a happy New Year,
And God send you a happy New Year.

Wassail, Wassail

18th Century Gloucestershire Carol

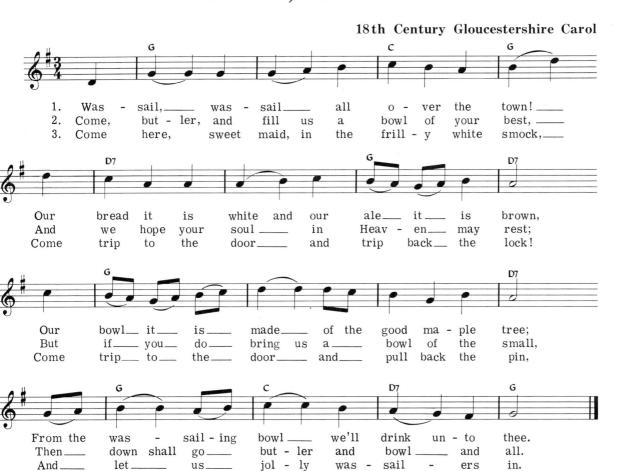

1. Was - sail, was - sail all o - ver the town!
2. Come, but - ler, and fill us a bowl of your best,
3. Come here, sweet maid, in the frill - y white smock,

Our bread it is white and our ale it is brown,
And we hope your soul in Heav - en may rest;
Come trip to the door and trip back the lock!

Our bowl it is made of the good ma - ple tree;
But if you do bring us a bowl of the small,
Come trip to the door and pull back the pin,

From the was - sail - ing bowl we'll drink un - to thee.
Then down shall go but - ler and bowl and all.
And let us jol - ly was - sail - ers in.

Water Come a' Me Eye

Caribbean Folk Song

Rhythmically

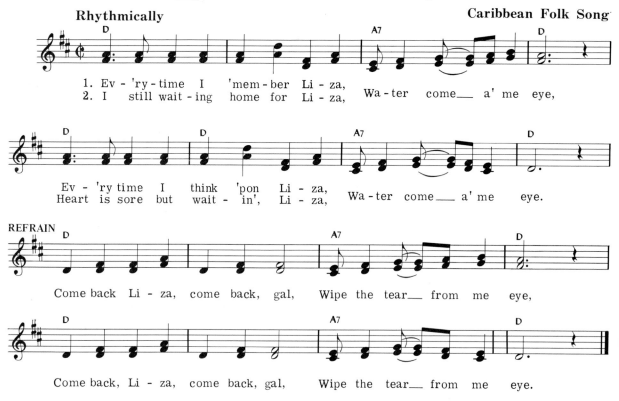

1. Ev - 'ry - time I 'mem - ber Li - za, Wa - ter come__ a' me eye,
2. I still wait - ing home for Li - za, Wa - ter come__ a' me eye,

Ev - 'ry time I think 'pon Li - za, Wa - ter come__ a' me eye.
Heart is sore but wait - in', Li - za, Wa - ter come__ a' me eye.

REFRAIN

Come back Li - za, come back, gal, Wipe the tear__ from me eye,

Come back, Li - za, come back, gal, Wipe the tear__ from me eye.

Add Calypso instruments for accompaniment.

Notice the harmony in parallel thirds below the melody. Encourage the children to find two places where fourths occur instead of thirds.

Weel May the Keel Row

Northumberland

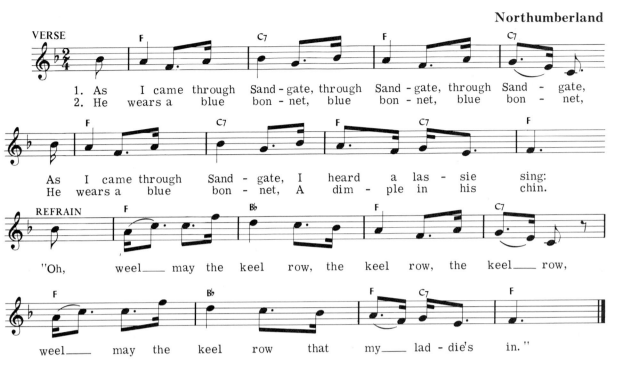

VERSE

1. As I came through Sand - gate, through Sand - gate, through Sand - gate,
2. He wears a blue bon - net, blue bon - net, blue bon - net,

As I came through Sand - gate, I heard a las - sie sing:
He wears a blue bon - net, A dim - ple in his chin.

REFRAIN

"Oh, weel___ may the keel row, the keel row, the keel___ row,

weel___ may the keel row that my___ lad - die's in."

2. He wears a blue bonnet, blue bonnet, blue bonnet,
   He wears a blue bonnet,
   A dimple in his chin.
   Oh, weel may the keel row, etc.

Play bagpipe bass on resonator bells, piano, or open strings of string bass.

Octave lower

Where Oh Where Is Pretty Little Susie?

1. Where oh where is pret-ty lit-tle Su - sie? Where oh where is pret-ty lit-tle Su - sie?
2. Come on, boys, let's go find her, Come on, boys, let's go find her,

Where oh where is pret-ty lit-tle Su - sie? Way down yon-der in the paw-paw patch.
Come on boys, let's go find her, Way down yon-der in the paw-paw patch.

This song may be sung as a partner song with "Bluebird," "He's Got the Whole World in His Hands" (H.S., p. 206), "Polly Put the Kettle On," "Rocka My Soul," "Sandy Land" (H.S., p. 107), "Skip to My Lou" (H.S., p. 232), and "Ten Little Indians" (H.S., p. 163).

The White Birch

Russian Folk Song
Words by P. H. Nielsen

Let me sing a song of the birch tree.

Stand - ing in the mea - dow is a birch tree

With its branch - es soft - ly sway - ing,

In the wind so gent - ly sway - ing.

This Russian folk song was used as the main theme for the fourth movement of Tchaikowsky's Symphony No. 4. The composer changes the theme in many ways for this theme and variations.

Who I Am

Easily

If an-y-bod-y asks you who I ___ am, ___
Who I ___ am, ___ Who I ___ am; ___
If an-y-bod-y asks you who I ___ am, ___
Tell them I'm a child of God.

On the last phrase, substitute the words, "Tell him I'm a boy named _____ or girl named _____ .

Who Killed Cock Robin?

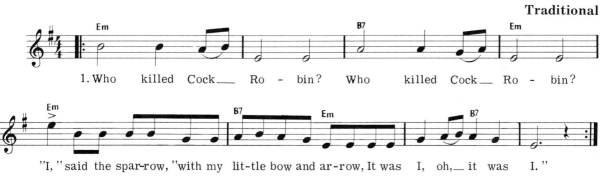

Traditional

1. Who killed Cock ___ Ro - bin? Who killed Cock ___ Ro - bin? "I," said the spar-row, "with my lit-tle bow and ar-row, It was I, oh, ___ it was I."

2. Who saw him die?
   "I," said the fly, "with my teency little eye."

3. Who made his cover?
   "I," said the beetle, "with my little sewing needle,"

4. Who dug his grave?
   "I," said the crow, "with my little spade and hoe,"

5. Who let him down?
   "I," said the crane, "with my little golden chain,"

6. Who filled his grave?
   "I," said the duck, "with my big old splatter foot,"

7. Who preached his funeral?
   "I," said the swallow, "just as loud as I could holler."

Note the octave leap between the first and second phrases.

Windy Weather

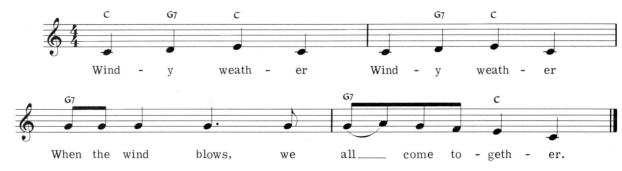

Wind - y weath - er Wind - y weath - er

When the wind blows, we all___ come to - geth - er.

Hand sign or play on melody instruments the following pattern each time it occurs.

Do Re Mi Do

Yonder She Comes

Missouri

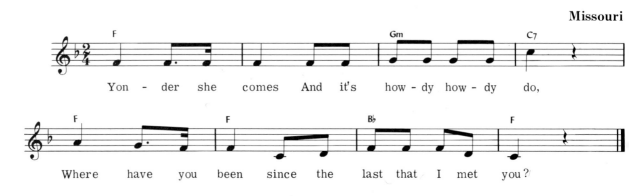

Yon - der she comes And it's how - dy how - dy do,

Where have you been since the last that I met you?

You Turn . . . I Turn

1. G

You turn for su-gar and tea, I turn for can - dy.

2. G *Fine*

Boys all love that su-gar and tea. Girls all love that can - dy.

3. G *D.C. al Fine*

You turn and I turn and You turn and I turn and

Try playing this pentatonic song on the notes G A B D E, or flat all notes and play on the black keys.

Sing in three-part round.

When adding pentatonic accompaniment do not chord.

Hine Ma Tov (A)

Text from Psalm 133 "How good and how pleasant it is for brethren to dwell together in unity."

Smoothly, not too fast   Israeli Round

1. Dm   Gm   Dm

Hi - ne ma tov u - ma na - im,

A7   Dm   *Fine*

she - vet a - chim gam ya - chad.

2. Dm   Gm   Dm

Hi - ne ma _____ tov,

A7   Dm   *D.C. al Fine*

she - vet a - chim gam ya - chad.

Yuletide is Here
Nu ä Jul Igen

Swedish Folk Song

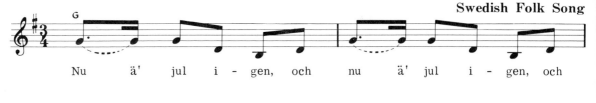

Nu ä' jul i - gen, och nu ä' jul i - gen, och

ju - len va - rar in - till pås - ka.

De' va' in - te sant och de' ve' in te sant, för

där - e - mel - lan kom - mer fas - ta.

English:

> Yuletide is here, oh Yuletide is here, oh
> Now the holly leaf is green-o.
> Easter would come when Yuletide is done if
> *Lent didn't fall between-o.

*Lent is a period of 40 days preceding Easter. In many Christian churches it is traditionally a time of fasting, a time for the members to make changes in their lives which will make them better persons and better followers of Christ. A habit or favorite item of food is often given up for this period of time.

This delightful English version was taught by rote to the author some years ago and its source is unknown.

Ziggy Za

Brazilian Singing Game

Es - cra - vo de Jo,   Jo - ga do no Ca - sen - ga.
Slave of the ja,   Throw it on ca - sen - ga.

Ti - ra,   bo - ta,   Del - xa fi - car.
Get it out,   Put it in,   Just let it be.

Guer - rei - ros com guer - rei - ros fa - zem zig - gy Zig - gy za.
The war - riors with wa - riors make zig - gy zig - gy za.

This Brazilian nonsense game is played with two players facing each other, seated. Each has a token of some kind (in Brazil they use small, empty match boxes) which he taps alternately in front of his partner and then in front of himself on the underlying beat of the song. The tapping is stopped, however, at the end of each phrase.

Alphabetical Index

Classified Index

ATONIC SONGS

PLAYING INSTRUMENTS

Keyboard

Percussion

Simple

tidatiatid   tara ti   timda   ti dam

2/4

Compound

6/

TRIP-ty   TRIP-le-ty   ta-a

4/4